NOWHERE TO HIDE

Jackie Randall

Dedication

Dedicated to the special people who inspired me to write my story, and to all the women and men who have suffered or are still suffering abuse.

****

24 HOUR SERVICE 1800 RESPECT

Australian National telephone and online counselling for people who have experience or are at risk of family and domestic and/or sexual assault.

http:www.1800respect.org.au/

FIRST EDITION

Book cover ©- Designed by BetiBup33 Design

ISBN: 978-0-646-84758-0

FORWARD

I live with the knowledge, heartache and pain that my husband murdered my mother, then shot me, before he turned the gun on himself.

To all the women and men who have lived with or are currently living with domestic violence, know you are not responsible for anyone's else's actions or reactions. However, it is up to you to get yourself away from the abuse. Please do so, before it's too late!

Your first step away will give you the strength to take the next one. We all think it will get better, but do not be like me and stay until it is too late. Twice!

My story is the unabashed truth but there is a deep need to protect the innocent, so names and places have been changed.

Judge me you may, but as you'll read, I have learned to live with worse than any harsh judgements and can only hope my story will help change other people's choices if the need arises.

You may find some of the content of my story distressing, but I can offer no apologies for what happened to me by others.

CONTENTS

Forward

NOWHERE TO HIDE

Jackie Randall

CHAPTER ONE

The Innocence of Yesterday

The story you are about to read, as unbelievable as it may sound, in that all these events could happen to one person is as true as a person's memory can recall. I know because I am that person with these horrendous memories.

Over the years I have lived my life over again and again in my thoughts and in my nightmares. I have told some of my story to people who are close to me, thus my life's events have become a script, entirely etched within my mind, and deeply burnt into my soul.

It is said time is a healer. The time for me to heal has arrived. To release myself from the past, the only way I can truly do that and as difficult as it is, is to write my story.

Many years have gone by since this all happened to me, and I want to share my story with you, so that if it can change or save even one person's life then my sharing this is more than worth it. All of it is the truth but, names and places are changed to protect the innocent.

To recall these events, I must re-live it and the words written are with burning raw emotions that bring back the very deep and painful memories. Seeing my words emerge on this paper is a cleanse from the past and sets me free to move into the future. Hopefully, it will set you free too in avoiding the very possible dire consequences of a life of abuse.

I want to start and to tell you first about my life with my parents. I feel my background is important to show you a part of my childhood and how my parents represented themselves to me. To demonstrate to you I came from a reasonably normal background in those days leading, for me, to what I believe a good life in my first eight years. I feel blessed and strengthened by the love of my parents.

My father saw his mother pass when he was ten-years old, and his father passed a year later. He was placed, with his brother, not much older than him, into the Church of England Boys' home. Later, through an agriculture programme, he was sponsored by a farmer and came out to Australia from England.

My Mother, at the tender age of three years was traumatized by the early death of her own mother and I believe this led to her to struggle with life choices.

When she was twenty-four, half Irish and half English and standing at barely five feet in height, she would slip into her size five shoe. Her petite build, dark curly hair, which softly framed her small face, full lips, and perfectly shaped hazel eyes, defined her beauty.

She paid her own way through college to become a professional seamstress, and always dressed immaculately. Dad, so smitten by her on first meeting, married mum within in the same year. Dad had apparently told Mum of his desire to have many children and had enough love for each one. This became very true.

I was the fifth born and there would be one more child to make six children. When I was a small baby Mum discovered a cheaper way to feed a baby, she would crush Milk Arrowroot biscuits with a rolling pin and place them in my bottle with warm Sunshine milk powder. This became my staple diet until one morning mum found me floppy and the doctor was called. It turned out I had soft bones due to a severe lack of nutrients in my diet and I was placed on one egg per day until I turned eight years old.

When I was seventeen months of age, I was sitting in my pram near the clothesline while Mum hung out the washing. The roo dog (used for hunting) from next door came into our yard and walked up to me whilst I was sitting in the pram. I raised my tiny arm to pat the dog, and it took one savage bite at my face. The bite left many teeth marks around my mouth. With the worst being a split that opened my top lip from the centre of my nose down through the lip. Mum held my lip together and ran to the hospital, which was a half mile away. She sat two hours continually holding my lip together with the both of us covered in my infant blood. The doctor didn't turn up, so Mum took me home because the blood had congealed and held my lip together.

Dad came home and was gutted to see my swollen ripped little face. He drove down to the police station making the police follow him back in the hope they would destroy the dog, but the neighbours had tied the dog up and said it had not left the yard. They moved to a new house soon after, taking the dog with them, but my scars on my face remained, to remind us all what that dog had done.

My Dad always called me a Gypsy because I used to wander away from home quite often, apparently as a toddler I had wandered off down the road but luckily, my Uncle Roger was the town postman and found me on his postie run. He placed me in the post-basket on his pushbike and took me back home as a special delivery. Another time I wandered off, I had been missing for two hours and eventually was found at a friend of my sisters' I went there because I liked the doll her friend had. I was able to borrow it for a while and we have a family portrait taken of me clutching the one and a half-legged doll that I so loved.

I can remember when I was three and my three older sisters took me to the beach close by where I slipped into the water. My sister thought it best to remove my wet undies to walk home. With help, I had to climb the picket but was feeling most embarrassed by the people in passing cars being able to see my private bits. It was ever so difficult to climb and try to pull my dress down to hide my naked bottom. This made me moody, and I gradually fell behind. We cut through an old cemetery and my leg fell through an old grave, I screamed out loud, "The devil has my leg!! He is pulling me down!!" I kept repeating these words until my three terrified sisters came back and pulled me free. I then snuggled into my eldest sister, who made me feel safe as she carried me all the way home.

One of my other nasty memories was about our toilet, it was an outhouse up the back yard, on top of the slope down to the house. There was a giant Berry-Thornbush right next to the toilet, the thorns were sharper than razor blades and I avoided it at all costs. I was about four years old and was terrified of going to the toilet. What was even scarier, was the septic tank in the ground, the lid had a crack that was at least an inch wide, it looked very dark down there and smell that wafted up was truly awful. One day I could hear my name being called from up the back yard, I went to see who it could be. It was Billy, one of my brother's eight-year-old friends. When I came within reach, he grabbed my arm, and led me to the septic tank. He made me stand on the lid near the crack, and I froze in terror of falling through.

Billy was yelling at me, "Take your pinny off or I will throw you in the thornbush." Terrified, I removed my pinny as I shook all over. He went through these threats until I was standing there naked wearing only my shoes and socks. I trembled in fear. I couldn't even stop my bottom lip from jiggling like it does when I am cold and shivering. My clothes were scattered over the -thorn bush as if they were laid out to dry. I couldn't reach them.

Billy just stood there pointing at my naked body laughing out loud then suddenly, he ran away.

Too scared to move, I started to scream and cry, Mum came running and taking off her apron, very tenderly wrapped it around my trembling body and carried me inside. She went back with the broom to collect my clothes from the thornbush. My family were outraged and promised to protect me, and this made me feel safe again. My loving Dad even cemented over the crack in the septic lid.

We moved to a bigger house just before my fifth birthday, the street was full of kids. Dad was loved by everyone, especially me. There were big families in our street and Dad would arrange soccer or cricket matches or football games out on our street. What fun we had. Every so often, on a payday Dad would come home early, load a bunch of us kids in the back of his work truck, and take us to get ice cream.

There was a time Dad was going to teach Mum to drive on Sunday afternoon. Some of us kids would pile in the little old Morris while Mum tried to learn to drive it. We weree on a back road where the sides of the road were edged with decent size rocks, mum seemed to line them up with one side of the car wheels and bounce along, with us kids in the back falling over each other and yelling to Dad to make her stop before we were all killed.

Mum gave up and brought a scooter, her first ride was in front of all our neighbours, they sat along the fence watching. Not sure if it made her nervous or gave her more determination, even so, she wobbled up the road but instead of steering it to turn it around, she leaned sideways, and Mum and scooter promptly fell over. Everyone laughed and clapped. Mum tried several more times, always with an audience, but she never managed to ride the scooter any better. The last time she fell over on the scooter, she stood up, put her head high in the air and walked home. Dad picked up the scooter and followed her. When he walked into the kitchen, Mum told Dad to sell the scooter, "I'm done," she said and never bothered with it again.

Both my parents loved playing sport, they both played tennis together and Dad was a coach for the local soccer team and also played a good game of cricket. Mum played badminton. One thing I remember is Mum wore canvas sports shoes and had to scrub them until they were green and then they were painted white, at night before bed she would place them in the wood-fuelled oven to dry. One morning I heard Mum scream, "Who shut the oven door?" We all ran into the kitchen thinking something dreadful had happened. Mum stood there, holding up her frizzled-up U-shaped sandshoes

Dad had shut the oven while there was still hot ash in the fireplace. We all ran outside, where we could better hide our laughter.

Soon after that, Dad bought some three-day-old chickens. The first night Dad was so worried they would be too cold in the chook pen, that we placed them in a box and put them in the open oven. Dad made sure we all knew they were there. In the morning, I heard Dad get up, so I raced to the kitchen so excited to see the chickens. The oven door was shut, as we took the box out, they were all dead, they had been cooked. Mum felt bad.

We didn't have a lot of money, but my life felt perfect, we had a wonderful family life and lots of laughter. My baby brother was born five months before I turned six, I was so super excited and became his little mummy, by the time he was eighteen months old I would take him to the Saturday afternoon matinee in his pusher, just him and me. I never had a problem doing so, he was the best little brother anyone could ever have. I would push him for two miles to get to the picture theatre and meet Dad afterward at the oval where he coached soccer.

My other brother, older by three years was born a 'blue baby,' the doctor. took too long to get him to breathe and consequently, my brother had minor brain damage.

Growing up with him was very annoying, as far back as memories go, he teased and tormented me. Mum would just say "When your father gets home, you will both get the strap."

Poor Dad would just walk in the door from work and Mum would say, "Les, take them out the back for the strap." My brother and I would run out the back and get under Dads' 1940's car that was quite high off the ground. We would see Dad pacing one side of the car and we would roll to the other side. Dad would reach out with the shaving strap and hit the ground. This was our game until he gave in and sent us back inside. We would get to the kitchen door and Dad would tell us to put our sad faces on, we would get the giggles and run through the kitchen.

One-night when I was seven years old, Dad came home from work and I ran to him, as usual, calling "Daddy," but somehow, this night Dad seemed different. He bent to me and told me to call him dad from now on because I was a big girl now. I went to mum and said there was something wrong with dad. It turned out Dad had advanced lung cancer. Our world with all the fun and laughter suddenly changed dramatically as we watched our father bed-ridden and slowing dying before us. He did his best to smile and joke, but our hearts were breaking. Mum was not coping very well and as I look back; I feel that I was forced to grow up with this difficult heart-breaking setback in slowly losing my loved father and trying to understand Mum's difficulty in coping. I was eight years old when I would regularly sit straddled across my father's chest lathering the soap to soften his whiskers and shaving his face with the cut-throat-razor. I enjoyed this special time, as I knew how much he trusted me. I have no regrets having to do this, as the love for my father was very special. The regret is that my father left my life too soon. For me, luckily my innocence did not allow me to understand fully what was happening to him.

Dad had such a strong will power, my eldest sister was about to marry, and Dad managed to walk her down the aisle. Halfway down the aisle, Dad's knee's buckled and he went down. People gasped and men stood to offer Dad support, but he waved them off and with a smile, he carried on. He even managed some time at the reception. In the following months, my sister told Dad he was going to be a grandfather and he vowed he would stay alive to meet his first grandchild, she was born on the sixth of July and Dad passed on the twentieth of July. This was the strength of my dad's willpower.

I remember how Dad stayed at home longer than the doctors recommended. It was the day he was struggling to breathe that Mum called the ambulance. It had been two years since his diagnosis, and I was ten years old when four of his six children lined the passageway to the door as they carried Dad out to the ambulance. He had propped himself up on one elbow and with a salute and a huge smile, he passed by us. This did make it less dramatic, but we were all speechless as our hearts were breaking, Mum would take us to the hospital as often as she could, and Dad always made jokes about himself.

The day came when we were told of our fifty-six-year-old father's passing. I know a very large part of me died that day with him. Mum refused to let me go to Dad's funeral and my young brother and I were dropped off at Mum's friend's house. I stayed outside on the far side of the house and cried forever. I was traumatised because all I wanted to do was say goodbye to Dad. That night Mum asked me to sleep on Dad's side of the bed which gave me a lot of comfort.

Sometime during the night, I awoke. My big toe was being squeezed and as I sat up, I saw an outline of Dad in a dark blue and bright green. He wore his biggest smile ever, and he was waving at me. I was so excited to see him and smiled back returning my biggest wave. Gradually the lines began to squiggle and move upwards while Dad remained smiling and waving in his ascension. I was so happy.

At breakfast, the next morning I felt excited to share my news about how Dad came to say goodbye, but mum became very cross and said it was just a dream and not to mention Dad ever again. My happiness in saying goodbye to Dad could not be dampened. I would tell my four-year-old brother wonderful stories about our dad to him, and he was always willing to listen.

The only thing that really helped, was going to school even though all the kids asked a million questions about what it like is to have a father who died.

CHAPTER TWO

Life with Mum

Mum, always concerned about money often took in male boarders. When I was twelve one of these boarders, who was at least six-foot-tall and in his early twenties seemed to think it was funny to tease and bully me. He would chase me around the house with a giant spider in a glass and one arm outstretched to grab the neck of my dress to drop the spider down. I ran as fast as I could squealing in fear. One day he managed to grab the back of my cotton dress by the neck as I was running. He ripped the whole back off leaving me with only the front half. I ran in the kitchen where Mum asked what happened to the back of my dress. On telling her the story she was angry my dress was damaged. "What about me," I asked, with her answer being "Try not to ruin your clothes." I felt dejected and that I was on my own with no backup.

Sometimes he would have a mouth full of petrol and ignite a cigarette lighter. When he was close enough, he would spray the petrol out of his mouth onto the lit lighter. This resulted in my fringe, eyebrows and eyelashes being singed off.

At dinner time if anything was left on my plate, he would wind the fine hairs on the back of my neck around his finger to hold my head over my plate forcing me to eat. I would call out to Mum to only see her run out the door. The more he got away with the more he tormented me, no one stood up to him. If the bath water was left in the bath, he would pick me up and drop me in the cold water at two am after coming back from the pub, my home life had become unbearable with no one to turn to.

Mum would just say she needed the money he paid for board. I felt somehow, I needed to do something, so one Friday I took his large rubber thongs and a big jam jar and went up to a paddock where there were sharp double gee's. They are a weed that have three sharp pronged needles in the seed that make you yelp when you step on one barefooted. I wore the thongs and pounded my feet over the sharp prickles then scraped them off into the jar. Once the jar was full, I raced home. I pulled back his bedding and sprinkled the jar of prickles all over the bottom sheet. I carefully remade the bed. I went to bed early and slept in Mum's bed waiting for him to return drunk from his night at the pub. I was woken by his screams and knew he had found the double gee's, I felt scared yet safe in Mum's bed and went to sleep with a smirk on my face.

The bullying continued and so I found a pair of Mum's old bra's and I stuffed them in one of his army reserve coat pockets and put two tennis balls in the other. He went off for the weekend on an army camp. Apparently, or so his story goes they were all sitting around the campfire when he put his hand in the pocket. Thinking it was a hankie he pulled it out revealing a big bra, his other hand pulled out the two tennis balls. All the Guys started laughing and teasing him, some asked if he was a cross-dresser. When he came back, he demanded to know how these items got into his pockets, but he was met with blank faces. I could hardly contain my smirk feeling extremely pleased with my ingenuity. He moved out soon after that, what a relief.

I worked hard at school and by the time I reached high school I was killing the good grades. Thinking about my future I decided I would go onto business college to become a private secretary and buy myself a convertible car…a life dream.

Finally knowing what I wanted in life, I told Mum about my goal, and she said as there was only my brother and I left at home now, I would be leaving school at fifteen to get a job to pay board to help her financially,

I pleaded with Mum to leave me at school and offered to get a job after school and weekends, my pleading fell on deaf ears.

The principal called me to the office as they received a letter stating I would leave school on my fifteenth birthday. I put my case forward and asked the principal to talk my Mum around. Mum stuck to her guns, so the principal said he was sorry that he failed.

Mum took me to see a friend of hers, who owned a hair salon where I was offered an apprenticeship, starting on two pounds a week. I refused and instead signed up at St John of Gods hospital to do my nurse training course on eight pounds per week.

I started training on the maternity ward aged fifteen and so very naïve. One of the nuns gave me a tour of the ward explaining my duties. The duty I feared most was if the red light came on above the delivery room door I was to go in and check on the mum-to-be.

I set about doing my duties and in between, I kept checking in case the red light came on. I had been in the nursery changing nappies on all the cute newborns and then went to see if the light had come on above the door of the delivery room and it was!

I rushed in and my first thought was, oh my goodness the baby's head was coming out the wrong hole! Mum had told me that babies came out from your bottom, and it was like having a hard poo. I managed to stay calm and said I would go and get the sister and hopefully, made her believe everything was okay even if I was in a panic and my brain is screaming: The baby is coming out of the wrong hole! I raced off down the corridor yelling for the sister and near knocked her over while I was still in a panic telling her to come quickly as the baby's head was poking out and she really needs urgent help.

I followed the sister into the ward, who very calmly told the lady everything was perfectly normal, and she was doing great and the baby was doing all the right things. My brain is like "What?" I had to go and get the doctor who was in the nursery and soon after, the baby was perfectly delivered without any complication. As soon as my shift was over, I practically ran all the way home to find Mum in the kitchen having a cup of tea as I burst out saying: "You lied to me! Babies don't come out of your bum." She simply smiled and sipped her tea.

We had to work in all the sections of the hospital, and I really enjoyed being in the Theatre with the doctors, I would get to put tonsils, appendix, and other things in jars. I learned a great deal more from the doctors, so I decided I wanted a career as a theatre nurse. After one year we would be sent to the city to work in the large hospital and stay in the nurse's quarters for two years training with the doctors after which, I would have my three stripes and become a qualified theatre nurse.

I was very excited, but because I was only sixteen, I had to have my mum's written permission. She refused. She told me she needed the board money and help around the house. Any chance to make a career for myself was gone. Two career blows, I gave up, thinking that living in a country town is not living the dream I expected.

I felt lost and alone, like back how I felt when Dad died. There were no options left. I had lost my dreams of a career, freedom and everything that went with it, and somehow, with it went my sparkle.

I took the first job that came along and existed from day to day. I kept questioning Mum about how I was supposed to find a career in a small town and her reply was always the same, "Girls get married, have babies with husbands who support them, and this is what you want." Although frustrated I could do nothing but give in, thankful I had some close friends who made life at least a little more bearable.

CHAPTER THREE

Marriage Love and Losses

One day I was introduced to Bernard, a friend's boyfriend. Wow, he was like something out of a movie. Tall, tanned, with a beautiful smile that would light up a room. He had warm blue eyes, blond hair and to top it off, denim flared jeans. Yes, this guy was hot. I thought how lucky my friend was.

Months later I was walking home from visiting my sister, and Bernard, who had broken off with my friend by then, pulled up in his car and offered to drive me home. On the way he asked me out and of course, I said yes.

When his knee touched mine, I felt electricity go through my whole body, after the first kiss I melted into a pool of liquid wax. Every time I looked into his eyes, I would stay locked there, I bumped into doors I was so love-struck, and this felt so incredible I knew I was in Love. Deeply and truly. All my emotions had exploded into one, I was in love and truly happy, this was the happiest I had been since before Dad became ill.

A year later, we were engaged to be married.

When I told mum, she was not at all happy. I was shocked at her reaction and asked why. Mum said she thought I would be different and make something of myself. I choked back the tears welling in my eyes as I looked into her eyes and replied. "I tried Mum, but you took away both my career choices and repeatedly told me this is what girls do." Judging by her face, I felt that this was the moment mum realised the consequences of the choices she made for me that bought us to this point. Now of course that is all in the past.

Bernard and I were married. It was a small family wedding where I met his mum and brothers for the first time. Life as Bernard's wife was filled with a lot of laughter and love.

Happy days

Soon enough, we were expecting our first child. We were both so excited. I moved back home to wait for the birth as Bernard was now working away at a construction camp, driving heavy machinery.

With six weeks to go we were so close to becoming parents, then one morning as I got out of bed, I was gripped by such an immense pain as I walked into the kitchen that I yelled out. Mum rushed in to see me doubled over and realised I had gone into premature labour. I panicked; it was far too early.

At the hospital, they said it was a false alarm and told mum to come back at lunchtime. As I lay there, the urge to push was intense and sudden, I was made to walk to the delivery room with no undies and a very short nighty on, the pain would make me double over and I knew my baby was not far off from being born. I begged the nuns to ring my doctor, they stalled, but soon enough it became obvious this baby was well and truly on his way. A nun grabbed the mask to put on me. I fought to push it away saying "No, I want to be awake!" The other nun came and held my hands, so the mask could be forced on. I began to drift into unconsciousness. I felt them roll me on my side cross my legs over and one lay on top of my legs to stop my baby boy from being born.

When I came to, my doctor was by my side, telling me my son had been born, but the silence in that room was eerily quiet. I jumped off the table running to find my baby son. There he lay, motionless, he had not even cried, his stomach was blue, they put a tube for oxygen in his nose. I knew he was in trouble. Before I could touch him the two nuns grabbed me by each arm and walked me to another room. A sleeping pill was slipped in my mouth. Over the next few days, I was kept sedated, where I remained in an impenetrable fog.

Mum had sent a telegram to Bernard to announce the early arrival of our precious baby son, the next day as new, terrified parents we had to wait at the viewing window to see our precious son. The nuns wheeled our baby boy over to the window in a Humidicrib, he laid there naked and perfect with his little display of blonde hair. Utter love poured from our hearts.

Bernard needed to go back down South to work, but as we kissed, we both felt overcome with joy and talked about taking our beautiful little boy home with us.

On the third day, one of the nuns came to get me as my baby had taken a bad turn. I rushed to the nursery, and nothing could prepare me for seeing my tiny son struggle for air as his little chest caved in and out. The doctor was there and shook his head, he placed a hand on my shoulder and said, "You know how it is," and walked off. If I hadn't been so paralysed by shock, I would have kicked the doctor in the butt! I refused the sleeping pills, so I could be with my baby boy. All I could do was reach in the humidicrib and stoke his chest and when I put my finger into his tiny palm, his fingers would curl around mine, "Hi," I would say, "I am your Mummy."

Sunday night baby Ralph was four days old and the gentlest nun in the hospital was with me as we both watched over him. She said he just needed to get through three more days, and he would be okay. He even cried, which is the first time I heard him cry. I cried with him. That night I went to sleep feeling hopeful, but at six o'clock in the morning, the nun standing by my bed, poked another sleeping pill in my mouth, and said my son had winged his way to heaven two hours earlier. As I slipped into sleep I could not grasp what she was saying. I awoke to feel my heart broken with the disbelief that my son was gone. I pressed the bell. I needed to see him. More than anything I needed to hold him. Feel him.

Say goodbye to him. They would not let me. I became engulfed in a despair of emotion so deep with disbelief I wasn't able to function. I became angry with the nuns. I blamed them for this nightmare I found myself engulfed in.

Mum came; she cried with me and said she would take care of everything. Our minister arrived and was talking about funeral arrangements. I cannot remember any of his words. All I could think about was how can they be burying my son? I was supposed to be taking him home!

Bernard arrived home that night. Standing at the front door in each other's arms, both heartbroken we cried. Wordlessly we clung to each other wishing for a different outcome. Not understanding why we lost our precious boy we shed tears of deep gut-wrenching grief.

I was so sedated, I couldn't stand, and I was unable to attend my beautiful baby boy's burial. My brother-in-law carried his little white coffin. My son was laid to rest, while I would carry the grief of losing him, forever.

CHAPTER FOUR

The Turning Point

The next eighteen months were unbearable, the nightmare would not end, and nothing made sense. I was on a planet that I did not fit in and didn't even really want to be on, but there was no escape.

I soon moved back to the town where Bernard was working. My grief ran so deep, that nothing seemed real anymore; nothing made sense. One minute I had a reasonably good marriage and was pregnant with our first child, the next I am childless and could hear people talking about Bernard's' drinking and going wild, having sex with other women, and all manner of debauchery. At this stage, I am not even sure that I cared about anything anymore.

One day Bernard came home with a puppy, and I started to come out of the nightmare I had been trapped in. He made me laugh again when one-night Bernard and I were watching TV, he had on flannel pyjamas and was telling me how his workmates said if you pass wind and hold a cigarette lighter lit near your butt it will make a blue flame. On saying this he put his knees near his ears, lit the lighter and let out a blast of air, it did ignite and was indeed a blue flame. Next minute he is whacking his pants, they were on fire, we laughed so hard and for the first time in a long time the laughing felt wonderful.

I fussed over the puppy and started to come back to a normal life, but it turned out my life was far from normal.

Bernard was drinking heavily and caused our laughter to stop. I also began to notice he showed signs of jealousy towards the puppy.

We moved back to my country hometown, desperate to return to our life before the tragedy of losing our son. We were staying at Mums' place when one time, Bernard came home from the pub at two o'clock in the morning. He came in smelling of alcohol and said, "You better go check your dog; I hit it over the head with a hammer." Shocked, I raced outside calling the puppy. I found the poor little thing with one side of its head twice the normal size. I spent the rest of the night cradling the dog and crying for her pain. In the morning, I reluctantly gave the dog to my mother for no other reason than to keep her safe from the brutality, inhumane and jealous actions of Bernard.

Bernard cried when I told him about what he had done to the dog. I felt sorry for him and covered it up to make him feel better and made an excuse for him telling him he did this out of his deep-seated grief over the loss of our son.

Sadly, life with Bernard didn't improve. Sure, there were days where it was fun, but the darker times grew in number and intensity. Our marriage began falling apart. I started going to church but this only made Bernard slip further into his darkness. One morning he slapped me so hard my bottom lip split, and blood poured down my chin. Five minutes later, he came back and saw my injury as if he had no idea about it. He cried when I told him he did the damage. He could not believe he had done this to me. He would buy me gifts, but the darkness would come back repeatedly, each time my injuries were worse and each time the same response from Bernard, crying in disbelief that he was responsible for my injuries.

The last straw came when he broke my nose.

I left him.

I told Mum what happened because there was no hiding a broken nose. Mum took immediate action and ushered me to a lawyer to start divorce papers, claiming, "Enough was more than enough."

It was during this time that my older brother was diagnosed with melanoma and given six weeks to live. I spent time being there for him and very much wanted Mum to tell my younger brother of the limited time we would have with our older brother, but she refused to let him know because he was studying at college. This choice would prove to have a lasting and detrimental effect on my young brother.

Bernard was devastated by this death and at my brother's funeral he clung to me and begged me to come back with all the promises of a loving happy marriage. I went back and yes; it was wonderful for six whole months. Then he began drinking again.

We returned to the construction camp and lived in a caravan. Because this was a job site, with a lot of employees, they made two camp sites: A and B camps. One Friday night, a payday, Bernard had gone to the pub straight after work as most of the guys would. I had a nice meal ready for him and as the time lapsed past our normal mealtime, I began to worry the food would go cold. I was putting rubbish in the bin outside when one of the work guys walked past. I asked him where Bernard was, and he said he was still at the pub taking bets that no matter how drunk or late he was, I would still have a warm meal waiting for him. I felt so hurt and humiliated that I placed his meal in the fridge and left a note on the table, it read: "Too late for a warm meal. Now in the fridge. Gone to visit Pat."

Pat, my best friend, had her caravan in B camp. I drove over to be with her for a little while to cool off. Sitting outside with Pat in the warm still night where you could hear a bird whistle off in the distance, was calming and serene. It didn't take long to breath in the peace and begin to relax. The small, sparsely populated country town nearby, consisted of a pub, a few shops and a small school with very few houses. farming surrounded the little town. I loved it out here.

In the quiet of the evening, I could hear Bernard's motorbike coming closer. He pulled up and walked towards us smiling. As I returned the smile, suddenly and without warning, I was the brunt of a vicious backhand across my cheek that tossed me over the edge of the chair. He turned and walked back to his bike, and I knew I was in real danger. I raced to the car and started it. Leaving the headlights off, I drove off into the darkness of the bush. I wound the window down, so I could hear his bike if it came close. I was so afraid of what he would do, so to escape his rage I kept driving in the dark. Ten minutes later, I realised I was at the back of our camp, so I parked the car in the bush and walked to Jack and Carol's caravan. I asked them if they had seen Bernard, they invited me inside, where they told me Bernard had ridden his bike back to the pub and rode it upstairs terrorising the guests then rode through the kitchen stealing two packs of steak. He was shouting how he was going to kill me when he found me. The police had been called. Suddenly we heard Bernard's bike approaching. Jack told me to hide in the bedroom. I laid flat like a mat on the floor and heard Bernard asking if they knew where I was because he was trying to find me so he could kill me. Both Jack and Carol said they didn't know where I was, and thankfully, he rode off.

Jack said he could see the police up at our van and some with torches scouring the bush, so I went up and introduced myself. The police shone their torch over me asking if I was all right. I said I was, that I was just frightened. They informed me they had him in the paddy van and were taking him to the lock up to protect me and that I needed to be at the courthouse at ten o'clock in the morning. I thought he would go to jail, but the judge called us both in and Bernard looked puzzled as to why he was there. The judge told him what he had done, and Bernard broke down in tears, so the Judge said he was banned from going to the local pub and how alcohol didn't mix with his brain chemicals. Bernard was full of remorse and promised to never touch alcohol again. So, I took him home. He quit his job and we moved to a new town, a new job and yes, a new pub.

It became easier to see when Bernard was edging towards one of his turns; his face would change; his eyes darkened and underwent a kind of vacant stare. His entire demeanour altered; he would become a stranger. He claimed the voices in his head needed to hurt me.

One Christmas eve, Bernard went out with friends. The next day we were to spend Christmas day with my mum. He asked me to pick him up from his mates' place in the morning. When I arrived on the Christmas morning to pick him up, I noticed that set expression and the darkness in his eyes. He grabbed my arm and jerked me out onto the road. Once on the road, he started spinning me around him. I had no control of which direction my body was being hurled. He glanced up to see a car heading our way and after a more powerful swing; he flung me to the road. I lay sprawled flat out on the bitumen, when luckily for me, the car turned into another direction. Frightened and shaking by this near miss, I got up and ran to our car to escape him. As I reached for the steering wheel to pull myself into the car, his boot slammed into my spine, not once, but time after agonising time.

Everything went quiet and he calmly told me to get in the car. I struggled in pain and bewilderment as to what could have brought on this vicious attack. Wondering what I had done wrong, I realised it was not me who had done the wrong, but that thought didn't help me feel any better.

As it turned out he had fractured my T6 vertebra. I was not able to get out of bed for a full three weeks.

To his credit, Bernard took time off work to look after me during this period of my recovery. He would shower me, take me to the toilet, and feed me. Bernard showed me how caring and loving he could be. Eventually I started to recover.

One night he bought a work-mate home for dinner because he felt sorry for him, because his wife had left him taking their two small young children with her. Doug was over six feet tall and had the saddest eyes, well-mannered and pleasant. I saw him around town from time to time and would always say hello. He eventually left to go back to the city to try for custody of the children.

Soon Bernard was back at the pub and so the beatings resumed. I lost count of the times I left him and would go back because of his promises of changing his behaviour. I loved the man I married, not this violent stranger who takes control of Bernard's brain. I had never told anyone of these terrifying events because I lived in hope that this stranger would leave and not come back, so that, when he went, I would have my Bernard back. I thought if I told anyone about him, they would turn on him and maybe make things worse. I was so very afraid of Bernard's dark side.

One night after his pub visit, Bernard bought a work colleague home, both of them were drunk and when Bernard passed out his mate tried to make a move on me. I threw his mate out and caught Bernard shutting his eyes. It was then I knew he had set me up. I was angry, something I would usually keep under control, but this was beyond that. As Bernard got up and moved towards me, I pushed past him and he lost his balance, his head hit the fridge. I turned around and saw that darkness coming over him and ran out the door. There were public toilets nearby, and I ran inside and locked the door. I crouched by the side of the toilet as rocks were being hurled through the above window. I was terrified a rock might land on my head and protected it the best I could when I heard him scream, "I'm so going to kill you this time."

The rocks and the screaming continued for at least twenty minutes, when suddenly there was complete silence. Out of the calmness came Bernard's voice. "Jackie, it's okay, you can come out, I will not harm you. It's me, Bernard." Hearing this I knew it was safe to come out from hiding. We walked home together, him holding my hand and saying the voices in his head were getting stronger and urged him to want to kill me. He felt, because the voices were getting so strong, he was losing control and conceded it would be safer to take me back to my mother's so she can keep me safe.

I knew he was being honest about this as this is the first time he told me about the voices in his head. We drove through the night, and he gently knocked on the door and when Mum answered, he calmly said, "Here is your daughter back, please look after her as I can't keep her safe anymore."

He kissed me and was gone.

Mum never said a word, she made up a bed for me and I cried myself to sleep.

CHAPTER FIVE

The Ultimatum

Three months passed since I had last seen or heard from Bernard. I secured a good job and bought a car. My younger brother and I bought ourselves motorbikes, so that on weekends we would go riding together with a group of nice friends. I was starting to feel happy and safe again and came to realise that Bernard had a mental problem and I had been living in fear of what he was capable of through his darkness. I felt completely free and knew I could never go back even though I still loved him.

It was a Saturday afternoon; there was a knock on the door. I opened it and was shocked, half scared, half pleased to see a smiling Bernard standing there. He leaned forward and very softly kissed my cheek whispering, "Hi, I've missed you." I found myself sink into his arms and felt the firmness of his chest and the smell of his aftershave that sent my senses into a frenzy of good memories.

Bernard had bought a new Kawasaki Z900 and offered to take me for a ride. The afternoon was carefree and fun, full of laughter and made me forget all the sadness and pain in the last five years. Four hours later, we said goodbye and he was gone.

Three weeks later Bernard showed up again. We spent another amazing afternoon together. This happened another three times, but this last time when saying goodbye, Bernard's face changed into that concrete look I feared and again I saw his darkness emerge. He looked me in the eyes and said, "Be my weekend wife or I will shoot you and then your mum. I will give you three weeks for your answer."

I do not know how long I stood there, paralysed in frozen fear. It seemed like just an instant of time between his saying goodbye and the flash of darkness that now crossed his face. The man with a severe mental problem had returned, only darker and heavier. Five years of abuse with numerous threats of killing me as well as the time he tried to kill my puppy and once when he grabbed the baby goats' legs and smashed her head repeatedly on the concrete before mercilessly throwing her limp body at my feet.

I could never go back living with that fear nor the horror he inflicted on defenceless animals when his darkness returned without provocation or warning. Not ever!

I went inside and told Mum about the ultimatum with three weeks to make a choice to be a weekend wife or for us to be shot. I ended up telling her everything that went on over the past five years of terror I endured and that I was not going back to another minute of it. Mum was amazing, she looked me in the eye and reassured me that Bernard would never carry out the threat of shooting us; she sealed my concern by saying things like, he didn't even own a gun, never shot one. She told me to put it out of my mind and stay strong. I decided to take her wise advice.

As the weeks passed, the trepidation of what loomed over me was getting heavier. My anxiety increased in not knowing if Bernard would come back for the answer he sought. The foreboding grew in intensity, and I told Mum I was going to go north and stay with friends for a while until Bernard got over his obsession. A friend had told me he was now living with a barmaid in Harvey. I had arranged to have my Kawasaki 400 serviced on the Monday before work. I planned to leave my car with Mum and on that Monday, I would hand in my immediate resignation and leave first thing the next day, a Tuesday. Wednesday was the day he said he would be back. Mum still did not believe it was necessary that I leave, but I noticed she was reading her bible a lot more. The apprehension, like a black cloud was descending, blacker and heavier. My whole being fought to ignore it. I failed. I had to listen to my instincts.

Monday came, I dropped my bike in for the service I had booked before work and had been given a small loan bike, a 150cc Suzuki road and trail bike. I set off for work and had only gone three hundred meters on the inside of three lanes of peak hour traffic, when a young girl drove through a stop sign as I approached. Even though I locked the brakes on, the light bike kept skidding forward. I dropped my body weight to one side in the hope of avoiding the car, but she had her eyes fixed on me in her revision mirror and followed me on the same path until there was nowhere left to go and we collided. The bike bounced up in the air and I knew my only chance was to hug the bike with my entire might and keep it straight for coming back down. As the bike landed back on the road, it fell away from me and I hit the road heavily on the right side of my body. I was sliding up the road waiting for my head to go under the car wheels in front of me. After what seemed like an eternity of sliding, I stopped. I tried to sit up, my head felt light, groggy, disorientated. My right arm was hanging in a weird position and I couldn't move it. I managed to get my full-face helmet off with my left arm. I looked up and saw the young girl walking towards me, crying and repeating, "I didn't see you."

I felt enraged! How was I going to carry out my plans of escaping Bernard now? I yelled at her and called her a stupid bitch. She ran back to the car crying. I couldn't move, three lanes of cars had come to a stop as the girl was parked in one, the bike laid on its side in the next and me, sitting there going nowhere. No one, not a soul came to help me, until a yellow RAC van pulled up on the medium strip and the driver came over. My hero, my rescuer. He asked if I needed ambulance or police. I told him I needed neither, because they would take too long. The pain was so intense, I couldn't wait so I said I just needed a lift to the hospital up the road a little further. He was amazing, he obtained all the details from the girl and told a passer-by to pick the bike up and stand it up against the pole off the road. He then carefully helped me up and got me into the front of the van. I winced. I could hardly breathe through the excruciating pain.

Once at the hospital he took control again, he rang my brother Harry to let him know what happened and where to pick the bike up with the bike trailer.

He gave me the details of the young girl and in between my gasps of pain. I thanked him sincerely and then he was gone. I didn't even get to know his name.

The right elbow joint had a fracture through and a deep abrasion to the top of the shoulder; I had skin off all my knuckles and damage to my right knee.

My right arm had a heavy plaster from my thumb to the upper arm and a sling to hold my arm in place. I was still in intense pain and when I was finally home, I needed Mum to undo and do up my jeans and help with dressing. Her tender care brought us even closer, and I loved her for it beyond words.

Tuesday, the day after the accident, I was in still in severe pain and by Wednesday morning, the pain became more intense. With the agony came the presentiment of the looming black cloud that felt like it was closing in on me. My gut instinct felt troubled with feelings of inexplicable fear, a tight curling of apprehension wrapped itself around my intestines and spiralled up my spine telling me there was a pending threat.

That evening Bernard knocked on the front door. He looked as though he was about to collapse when he saw all my injuries and appeared upset that we didn't notify him, he was clearly very distressed. Out of the goodness of his heart, he then told me he would give me a further seven days for my answer and was gone.

Mum continued to reassure me that nothing would come of it. I didn't feel very reassured at all. That gnawing feeling of danger kept churning in my stomach. I couldn't shake it.

One day, not long after Bernard's offer to extend the time on the ultimatum, Mum brought out her special tin that contained her own hand-written will. In it she stated she would like my older brother's grave to be opened, and for her to be buried with her child. Speaking of what to do when she passes was so hard to hear, but it was important to her and so I listened. She felt her time was very near as in the last six months or more, my mum suffered constant diarrhoea, tests revealed the likelihood of the start of bowel cancer. Mum felt very fearful of a slow suffering death and said she would pray every night for a quick end without suffering. She said that after watching my dad suffer for two years, dying of cancer, then my older brother, she could not bear to suffer. She wanted to have everything in order. Then she made me promise her, no matter what, that I would look after my younger brother who was now nineteen. I was twenty-five. I promised I would, no matter what happened. This seemed to give her a greater sense of peace.

She put the tin away and then bought out something wrapped in white tissue paper. As she unfolded it, she looked at me tenderly and said, "I truly believe the day will come where you will have two little daughters, so I have knitted this baby pink dress with matching bonnet and booties for them. We cried together in that special and sensitive moment. I held the little outfit my mother made for my future daughters to my face as tears spilled onto the gorgeous set of hand-knitted clothes.

The black cloud pressed down on me all that day. The feeling of doom felt stronger than ever, I talked to Mum about it, but she dismissed it and told me it was because of the bike accident and the ongoing pain I was in. I felt helpless, with no place to turn.

CHAPTER SIX

That Fateful Day

Bernard turned up during the evening of that Wednesday; his breath reeked of rum. He appeared calm; my gut churned even through his small talk. He had been there for about forty minutes, then asked me for my decision on being his weekend wife. Somehow, and I can't fully explain why, I felt more relaxed, perhaps because Bernard had remained calm, unperturbed and pleasant through the small talk. I went on to tell him he needed medical help, I would be there to support him all the way, and then we could look at the future but not until then. He took it well and responded by saying, "So that is your decision." I repeated that I would stand by him if he sought medical help for the voices in his head. His calm demeanour didn't alter as we continued small talk for about another ten minutes. He then said that friends were leaving town and he needed to go and say goodbye to them, but could he come back and see me. I replied that he was always welcome.

I didn't worry about locking the front door behind him because he intended to return soon.

I sat back into the single lounge chair, my plastered arm resting across my chest. My pet budgie lay asleep on my plaster, his little head nestled in his fluffed feathers. My brother sat on the three-seater next to me, and Mum sat laid back in the other single lounge chair. We were watching TV and relaxing when the front door opened.

Bernard walked in with a towel draped over a long object in his hand. When he came level to me, he pulled the towel off to reveal a .22 rifle

As he raised the gun to point towards me, I tried to stand, by leaning on my left hand to lever myself up when I heard his words, "I told you, I would take you with me," he said.

Before I could move any further, I felt the bullet blow right through my chest and out through the shoulder blade. I felt no immediate pain, just a rush of air whooshing from out of me as my body lurched forward and then backward. My head dropped and I watched as my blood spurted from my chest. My brain screamed, "I have really been shot!"

Things felt surreal. This wasn't happening and as if in slow motion, I looked up and watched as Bernard stepped towards Mum. The rifle now pointing at her. Panic filled me as I pleaded with him to stop. My eyes travelled to Mum and the expression of utter shock and disbelief crossed her face as another shot filled the air. Mum slumped in her chair; blood oozed from her mortal wound.

Bernard turned the gun around and pointed it at my head. I could do nothing but plead with him. My young brother stood up in front of Bernard, the gun now pointed in his stomach, their eyes locked. An overwhelming dread filled me, and I willed my brother to sit down, more than anything I needed him to be spared. Only three weeks ago, I had promised if anything ever happened to Mum, I would take care of him. I sincerely made that promise. I sincerely wanted him to stay safe from Bernard's next shot. It was all that filed my mind at that moment.

Nothing would stop Bernard now, I certainly could not, but thankfully, my nineteen-year-old brother heeded my internal pleas and backed down to take his seat. Again, the gun swung and pointed at my head. I was sitting up and knew I would not survive a bullet in the head, he fired the gun, the bullet passed through my fringe I felt the bullet lift my hair.

Instincts took over and I slumped back in the chair. I could hear my brain sending frantic messages, do not open your eyes. Don't even blink. Do not show signs of breathing. Move nothing, act as if you are truly dead. I sensed Bernard walk to stand in front of me. The gun aimed right at me; it felt like that moment to pass, before he shot me for the last time, was taking forever.

The gun went off and there was a thud to the floor. I knew it was Bernard. I opened my eyes and there he was, crumpled to the floor in front of me, blood oozing from the self-inflicted gunshot to the side of his head.

He was dead. I felt all the terror had finally ended, died with him. A strange sense of relief flooded through me.

Because Mum had never had the phone connected, Harry ran next door to call an ambulance. I looked over at Mum, she remained still and unmoving in the same slumped position, and she was dying. I knew and I believe she did too.

Mum was a very devout believer in God and so I knew she would want me to pray for her. As I was praying to God to forgive her for any sins not covered in her own prayers, and accept her into his Kingdom, I noticed a gold light in the corner of the room that spread quickly across the ceiling. The light began to descend until it became level with my face. An incredible warmth enveloped me, a warmth that seemed to fill me with unconditional love and an inexplicable feeling of peace. The event felt unlike anything I had ever experienced before and permeated my entire being. A voice, yet not a voice, more a knowing, a different kind of communication filled my mind. The sound was more beautiful than any human utterances had ever resounded in my ears. The voice said "Jackie, do you want to come?"

I instinctively knew what was being asked. Oh Yes, I wanted to go to the warmth, the love, and forever feel the great depth of peace, and be with my mum. At that moment, though, I remembered the promise I had made to Mum in being here to care for Harry.

I had to stay.

I whispered.

"I can't go."

CHAPTER SEVEN

I Chose to Live

"POOF" the golden window closed. Mum took her last breath and an extreme agony set in at that very moment. There is no one-to-ten measuring the level of pain, as mine was sitting at an excruciating level.

Harry came back and knelt near me, I tried to tell him I was here to stay and look after him, I had been given a choice and I chose to keep my promise, but I was incoherent, and he never heard my words' I was still saying I'm not going to die. All he heard was me repeating the word die.

The detectives were the first to arrive, one younger and the one in his forties, he was so matter of fact even callous with little to no empathy as he took out his notebook and pen with no eye contact until he looked at my brother and asked," What is your girlfriends name?"

My poor brother was shaking as anger now stirred in him and pointing to me saying with a shaky voice," "That is my sister and that is my mother and that is my brother in-law." he pointed to each of us in turn. The younger Detective started to sob and the older one went quiet.

An ambulance officer came in and instantly ran back out the door. I started to panic, I was eyeballing everyone, but by now could not get words out. Then the ambulance officer leaning over the balcony on the fourth floor where we were, yelled, "Only need one stretcher," it was horrible to think I was hoping it was for me because I knew both Mum and Bernard had passed away.

The ambulance Officer's came in with the stretcher, and they were very carefully transferring me onto the stretcher, but I was trying desperately to tell them that the air was escaping out through the hole in my shoulder blade, I was quite distressed and could only try to put my hand over the right shoulder. They soon realised what I was trying to tell them and placed a cushion under it, which did make a difference.

They kept asking me my name, I continuously repeated, "Jackie Randall". I was feeling annoyed as it appeared, they did not hear me. I was being placed in the ambulance when I heard a male sobbing and the older detective reassuring my brother that he will be okay and just sit in the car. I felt some comfort knowing Harry would be coming with me.

The ambulance officer who was in the back with me was so lovely and caring, he smiled and was taking my pulse when he suddenly called out to the driver, "We are losing her, call for police escort and man all intersections from here to the hospital. Priority One!!" he yelled

My eyes were starting to roll, I was not afraid, I knew I would live. I heard the police bikes and their sirens as they raced in front of the Ambulance, I wanted to sit up and have a look, but by now, there was no energy left to even flick a finger.

When I was being taken out of the ambulance my eyes were still rolling, I could see a lot of hospital staff all lined up waiting for me. I was rushed into emergency and could count eight people around me; I was propped in a half sitting position because I was drowning in my own blood. The head surgeon was telling me they needed to put a syringe in through my back into my lung to quickly drain some blood out, so I could breathe a bit easier. I was already in acute pain so at that point what was a bit more pain and I knew they were working to save my life. The .22 bullet had entered my chest and missed my heart by 2.5cm then split the fifth rib, from there it travelled through my lung which caused it to collapse and bleed. The bullet then exited out through my right shoulder blade.

Someone was removing all my clothes; my black knitted top was cut down the back for easier removal. I was naked with a room full of people, but somehow it just did not matter. I knew they were all there working as a team to save my life. The amazing thing was that even though I could not talk I was hearing eight conversations clearly and aware of what each one was doing. A doctor was trying to find a vein to draw blood to identify my blood group and it seemed the only place he found a surface vein was near my ankle. Meanwhile a young doctor was trying to put a drip line in my neck, he had four goes and I found the strength to talk and asked him to give up because he was hurting me. I saw him walk over to the wall and sob, he was the one who cared the most, and I felt awful for upsetting him.

The surgeon went over and brought him back instructing him to follow where the main artery would run down my neck and try again. This time he was successful. At the same time someone was also putting a line into the back of my left hand, so they could start the blood drip to replace the massive amount of blood I had already lost.

The surgeon was now by my side telling me they would have to cut between my ribs through the lung, so a drainage tube could be inserted to drain the blood. I nodded, as I understood what he was, saying however I was not prepared for the most severe physical pain you could imagine when the scalpel started to cut through my skin. I screamed loudly, my right arm that had been lifeless in the heavy cast for the past ten days since the motorbike accident suddenly moved with my left hand, I grabbed the doctors' hand with the scalpel pulling it above my chest.

The nice young doctor who had been cradling my head in his arms asked the surgeon to give me something for the pain, but he responded by saying my veins would all collapse due to the massive blood loss and I would die. My only chance to survive was to fight. It took four people to hold me down while he cut through to my lung and a tube was pushed through the cut, it felt like a meter of hose going in and then the opening was stitched around the tube to close it.

I felt my lips and it was like a seal forming over them, I ripped it off as I felt it was a sign of death approaching, I asked for a drink of water and was allowed a sip only. I asked for my brother as it had been three hours since I had arrived and thought my brother was sitting outside waiting, unknown to me he had only just arrived at the hospital and came in with the two detectives.

The surgeon was telling the Detectives they needed to notify all my family, so they could try to get here to say goodbye, as they did not believe I would make it through the night. By this stage I was now so exhausted I could only blink.

It gave me great comfort to finally see Harry, just a pity I was unable to speak and tell him I was going to live but at least they had put a sheet over my naked body.

CHAPTER EIGHT

My Fight for Survival

The nurse wheeled me on a trolley through heavy plastic doors, the air felt cool then I saw the rows of beds where each had a white sheet like I did. People lay there stiff and quiet their feet together and pointing up to the ceiling. I was placed at the end of the row on the left. A sudden terror gripped me like a vice!

I wanted to flap my arms and kick my legs, even scream out to tell then, I'm alive! Don't leave me here in the morgue! Panic wrapped it's tendrils around me because all I could do was blink my eyes and hope someone noticed. Nothing. The nurse placed a chair next to my bed and started to read her book. I was too scared to fall asleep as they might think I am dead, but I must have fallen asleep because I woke with such a strong flick of my eye lids, the nurse leaped out of her chair. I looked her in the eyes, and she merely sat down and continued reading her book.

Next time I woke it was morning and at the foot of my bed was the nice doctor who had cradled my head. I told him to get me out of this morgue. He gave a little laugh and said, "We're moving you out of here, you are way too healthy to be here." He told me I was actually in the ICU (Intensive Care Unit) where I was being monitored so not the morgue after all.

He wheeled me to a private room with a small window that looked at the wall of a red-bricked building. A smiling male nurse came in and I heard myself say. "I have been shot," It appeared my brain was trying to convince itself of the reality of what had happened. The male nurse smiled and said, "You're safe now, I'm here to look after you."

The day was a bit of a blur, except for all the doctors and nursing staff coming and going. At one point, they wheeled in an X-ray machine and when they propped me up, I let out a dreadful gasp, as the pain shot through my chest, and I struggled to breathe. My right fifth rib had been split by the bullet and created such intense pain and my lung that had collapsed was still bleeding but draining well through the inserted tube in my lung. I was still connected to so many tubes. I received six packs of blood to replace what I had lost. At least the penicillin was injected into the drip line.

The second night was a rough one as the pain became unbearable and was given an injection of morphine. It was then they told me I had not passed urine in the last thirty hours because my organs had begun to shut down. I was told that if I didn't pass any in the next few hours a catheter would be inserted.

They brought in a cold bedpan, two nursing staff assisted me to a sitting position, and at that moment I vomited all over the bed quilt. A disgusting mass of gross pinkish lumps from the blood that had poured out and gone into my stomach lay all over my lap. The sight of it made me vomit even more.

I was propped on the cold bedpan with staff encouraging me to pee, someone turned on a trickling tap and finally a very small amount of urine passed. A celebration ensued with shouts of praise and clapping. I felt very pleased with myself.

Morning came, hospital staff still in and out all doing their tasks, then a detective came, he sat so close to my bed, his face close to mine as he softly introduced himself and ask if I was up to answering just a couple of questions, or he could come back another time. I was eager to get it over and done with, he had a very pleasant face, and his eyes were filled with compassion when he said, "I just want you to know that you are not responsible for anyone else's actions."

They were the words I so needed to hear, and words I still carry around in my heart to this day, reminding me, Gerard's actions were not my fault. These few words caused me to feel all the misdirected guilt lift out from within me. I cried.

Throughout the day, family came to visit, and I felt their grief and compassion with absolutely no blame for what Gerard had done. We all knew he was mentally ill.

Every day they would wheel in the Xray machine for results, to see what was happening with my lung. Someone would lay me flat, and a spirit level was placed across my chest, this freaked me out as I thought he was measuring me up for a coffin, until he explained they were waiting for my right lung to self-inflate, but it had not. The surgeon came in and as he moved his finger on a line where he would cut, said I needed to breathe deeper to help the lung to inflate otherwise they would have to remove it and cut me open from front to back and rip my collapsed lung out. I felt sure he only meant to scare me but let me tell you, it worked. I pushed through incredibly intense pain as I tried to breathe as deep as the pain would allow. I kept it up for as omg as I could.

Day 3. My lovely male nurse entered the room calling out, "Hello Sunshine." I had to place my hands over my ears as the noise was really hurting my ears and the sound of his loud footsteps, he turned on the air-condition (it was the end of a Hot February) and the sound was as if a jumbo jet had started up in my room. "Turn it off!" I repeated through clenched teeth. The male nurse ran over placed his fingers each side of my mouth telling me to open my mouth, but I could not, so he pressed the emergency button and the head surgeon, and several others flooded into my room. By this time the muscles in my whole body were going into spasms. I felt the bed sliding back and forward with the seizure's and soon they placed me on oxygen. Again, I heard the surgeon say, "We are losing her, we can't save her this time."

I was begging them to rub my painful muscles. The surgeon said I had tetanus; my last vaccine was only 2 years earlier, when the bullet entered my chest, apparently the bullet pulled in fibres from the knitted top I was wearing at the time.

Saturday at 11am, I remember a feeling entering the top of my head and sweeping through my whole body right to my toes. It felt like something really bad was literally flung out of me, I sat up. Clearly and calmly I announced, "Thank you I am alright now."

Everyone in the room leaned back in disbelief, but truly, I was fine.

Unbeknownst to me at that same time, my family were saying prayers for me amid a group of 2,000 other church people

The hospital staff stood there in stunned silence and after checking me over found, I was indeed all right.

I can only put it down to the power of prayer.

CHAPTER NINE

The long Road to Healing

Day 4. The nurse had given me penicillin through my drip line, and I was looking at the underneath of my forearms watching a rash developing quite rapidly so I called out to the nurse who was in the room with me and again the emergency button was pushed. I was having a severe reaction to the penicillin and had to receive another injection to try and control the allergic reaction. I swelled up all over and could have signed up for the Michelin tyre advertisement on TV.

One of the daily smiles I had was through a patient with mild dementia who had received open heart surgery. When he was well enough to walk the corridor, and he passed my door, I saw he was entirely naked except for the staples down his chest, painted red with mercurochrome. He became known as flash Gordon. Every day he would do a naked run with arms waving high in the air. It did make me giggle.

Day 5. The daily Xray was taken, the physio with his spirit level (still freaked me out.) The surgeon was there, and he was pleased with me as the right lung was showing signs of improving. I used a ceramic pot of steam to breathe in but after that was a machine called the birdie which had a tube and was put in my mouth. The air from this rushed down to my lungs and I was to push the air back out making both my lungs work hard. I now know how a balloon feels like when they are being filled with air and it is trapped in there. The big problem was my fifth rib, which had been split by the bullet when the air was expanding my lung pushing my rib cage out, causing that high level of pain I had to push through. They tried this machine a few times but gave up because of the threshold of intense pain going over and beyond the limit of endurance.

People came to visit, I was not always aware of who had come to visit, some were family to discuss what funeral arrangement had been made for Mum on day seven and Bernard's family came from over East to plan a cremation service on day eight. They wanted to take his ashes back with them although they did offer me half of his ashes. My traumatised brain wanted to ask what half I would get. However, I was able to sincerely thank them, but would rather they take him back whole.

Some visitors were family of friends; they would just sit there, say hello with very few other words and just stare at me as if they were waiting to see if I was going to die at that moment. Made me feel uncomfortable. I also realise there had been no talk, like I was ever going to leave this place. When alone there was only the walls to stare at, or the brick wall out the window and Flash Gordon doing his daily run.

The staff of the ICU were amazing and so protective of me, they would make sure, no newspapers would come into my room, even though reporters tried, the staff kept them away. I would always be asked if I wanted to see who ever was there to visit me. Only a few visitors at a time as I tired very easily. Then one morning they asked if I wanted to see Doug, the man who had come for dinner about nine months before. He stood in the doorway of my hospital room. His lean, 6'2" build held a beautiful bunch of pale pink carnations, the only flowers I received that I was aware of. When he lowered the flowers from in front of his face, he had a lovely cheeky smile, he made me laugh. It hurt, but it felt so good to laugh. He sat and e chatted away about life outside of here and of his two children. He said he had read about what had happened in the newspaper and remembered how kind I was to him the night he came to dinner. When it was time for him to leave, he wrote his phone number on my plaster that was still on my right arm and told me to ring him when I was ready to go out and have a cup of coffee.

I started to think more of my brother and the urge to get out of the hospital and be with him and the land of the living. Harry had told me that the unit we lived in needed to be cleared out, as we were moving into a flat that had been arranged for us, our friends had agreed to help him with a couple of utes.

It was the day of Mums' funeral; I was still too unwell to attend. It made me feel like the walls of my room were closing in on me. Next day was Bernard's cremation. Even if I was well enough, I wouldn't have gone. I already said goodbye after he fired the last bullet and he lay dying at my feet.

The day they cremated Bernard; was also the day they removed all the tubes from my body. This simple procedure felt like freedom towards a new life. I asked the surgeon about being released from the hospital, but he went on to say it would be a stay of between four to six weeks due to a possibility of a second bleed or the collapse of my right lung. I promised to come back every day if he would just let me go. To which he replied that they were also concerned that I had not reacted to what had happened. He said he would send up a psychiatrist.

She came that afternoon and said they were worried I had not reacted enough to the trauma of the shooting. I explained that my Mum said she was scared she would suffer and die slowly from bowel cancer and would not be able to bear it. She wanted a very quick end to her life. I felt in a way, for me to deal with her sudden death, that being shot was almost like she got her wish, and this made me feel better in a way that she didn't have to suffer a death by a slow killing cancer. As for Bernard, his nightmare was over, and I would not have to live in fear ever again.

I told the psychiatrist I needed to be with my brother to care for him. I was worried that he was the one who dealt with the real reality of all that happened. The police took him to the station first to question him, then to face the family, they should have kept him in the hospital with me, even for a couple of days, just so he would also feel protected.

She still felt it was not enough, so I told her to get two bricks and I would run around the hospital and smash windows. Once I did this, I asked if this was going to be enough 'dealing' with the problem and then could I go. To my surprise, she laughed aloud and with a huge smile, she said I could go.

Ten days of being in ICU, I could go on the promise I would come for daily check-ups over the next two weeks. My brother came to pick me up and I managed to walk out on shaky legs, I had lost over seven kilos, down to 43k.

Stepping out onto the street the smell of fresh air was glorious and I took a deep breath and knew I was back in the land of the living.

Driving away from the hospital with my brother at the wheel, I thought we were driving into the future of new beginnings, I felt a sense of relief and a small smile on my lips but there was still more horror to come that I was not remotely prepared for.

Harry was telling me we had to go to Mums unit and pack it up before we could go to our new apartment. The coldest chill went through my spine and left me speechless, "Where are the family?" I quietly asked trying to hide the fear escalating through me, I had not thought about this, going back to where I was shot, to where death took place. Mum murdered by my husband who then shot himself in the head and died in front of me. I just couldn't face this. Not now. Not ever!

Harry said the family had gone back to their hometown, but three of our friends were meeting us there.

Nothing could prepare me for what I was about to face, I made Harry promise me he would stay by my side every second. I got to the front door and as I entered, the stench of death knocked me backward, I wanted to run and scream and just yell, "No!!"

My whole being became numb.

Feeling traumatised beyond belief; I followed Harry into the lounge where it all happened. As I write this, my head is fuzzy, and the base of my skull has tensed, my heart has almost gone silent as I recall these moments. In hospital I was protected, cared for and nurtured, but now, I stood where it happened and re-lived every second. I saw Bernard's blood stain on the carpet where he died. The chair with Mum's blood, I wanted to touch it, my mind trying to deal with the fact that it all really did happen.

I am in front of the chair where I had sat, my blood on the cushion and the hole where the bullet entered the couch after exiting my body. I looked at the wall and saw the bullet hole that was meant for my head. I started to panic, and there was no air to breathe. I ran into the laundry looking for Harry, all I found was mum's blood-stained dress that she had been wearing, now in the laundry basin.

Stark horror gripped me, and I ran back into the lounge only to find my mother's glasses and false teeth on the side table where she had sat.

I started to scream for Harry and ran out the front door in a blind panic. My poor weakened body could no longer support me, and I started to drop to the ground.

The building manager had appeared and grabbed me to support me upright. "What in the hell are you doing here Jackie?" it was said with shock and empathy. I mumbled that we were told to clear the unit, but I pleaded that I could not go back in. At that moment I wanted to be back in my hospital room with my nurse calling me Sunshine and feeling safe, protected and nurtured and realized I had not been as ready as I thought, to have been released.

The building manager was amazing and said he would take care of everything. Harry told him what was our personal belongings that we needed, and the manager was leading me towards the lift. I was in shock, words were frozen.

Next minute we were in his office, and he handed me my pet budgie in his cage. My beautiful budgerigar chirped me a greeting. "Hello pretty boy," I said as tears fell. I realised this was the first time I had cried since the shooting. This kind wonderful man had rescued my bird that had been sitting on my cast when I was shot. I managed to thank him from my heart and gave him a hug. He said he would miss the bird so as a thank you I left the bird with him for going out of his way to help us.

Harry had come in from loading our personal belongings into the back of his friend's ute. We

drove away from there knowing we were never going back.

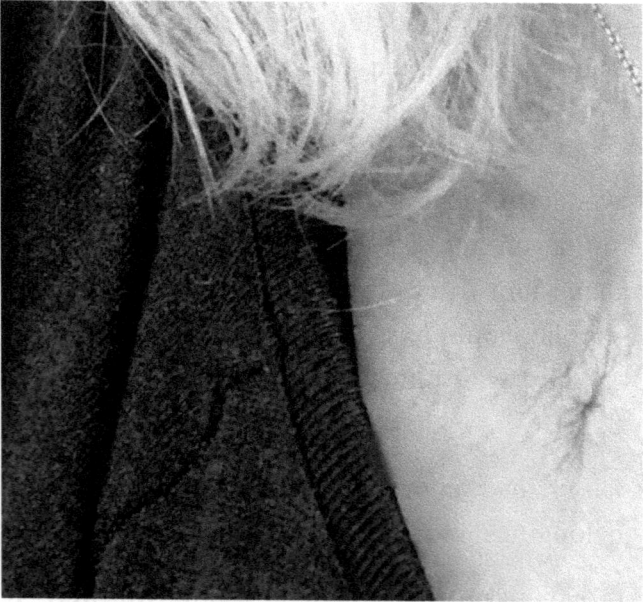

Marked for life.

A stark reminder of that fateful day.

CHAPTER TEN

Mental and Physical Scars

Events from there became a bit of a blur for a while as we struggled to fit into some sort of normal life. It was easier to hide amongst strangers in the big city and with the support of our wonderful friends, we relaxed a little. I don't know how long it took before either of us slept in our beds. we purchased a black bean bag lounge, two single and one double. Our snuggle chairs as they became known as, gave us some semblance of comfort.

It had been a month since the shooting and we decided to take a trip to the country to see family, we stayed with my sister and her husband. When I walked into their lounge it felt like nothing had ever happened. No reference to the shooting, my hospital stay or any of the trauma we suffered was aired. I chose not to say anything.

The next day we were walking down the main street of the shopping area and a friend of the family stopped before she passed us by and said, "Hi Jackie, I read what happened in the newspaper, dreadful thing. Oh, is that where you got shot!"

As she neared, she poked at me where I had the drain tube removed. Well, she could have kicked me hard in the shins and it would not have hurt as much as her words. I was so shaken we went back to the house. This is the town we were all born in and lived. A little bit of decorum might have gone a long way towards my healing. This attitude made me feel an urgent need to go back to the city as soon as possible where people were strangers and my life less on show for the pokers and the curious and the melodramatic, who held no real compassion in their hearts. I thought it better to be inconspicuous rather than a talking piece.

The police came to give me all that Bernard owned. Just a suitcase full, and they stayed while I opened it, which I was grateful for. I could not have done it otherwise. It contained mainly clothes and miscellaneous items, there was a life insurance but of course it was made void due to his suicide. The Detective appeared embarrassed as he handed me an envelope with $13.25 inside, all Bernard had to show for the twenty-eight years of his life. I later threw it all in the rubbish bin. The Detective went on to say they had impounded his Kawasaki Z900 motorbike and what did I want to do with it, there were papers in the suitcase to show that Bernard had borrowed the money from the bank to purchase it. I told the police to keep it there and I would contact the bank.

When I went to see the bank manager, he was quite rude and started to tell me I was responsible for the debt and only one payment was made, by the time I finished giving him my story he was more understanding, I was in tears and here I was still dealing with Bernard's problems even after his death. The bank manager said he would arrange for the bike to be auctioned off. Later I was informed there was no money left owing.

The Detective had also told me the rifle Bernard used was swapped by him for our colour TV. The poor guy who owned the rifle was well known in a small town south of the city for always helping others out and was heavily involved in charity work. A Family man. Bernard told him the rifle would be used for shooting rabbits. The bloke collapsed when the police had told him what happened, and that Bernard didn't have a gun licence. The person felt gutted and told the police to pass onto me how sorry he was. The Detective went on to say I could press charges against him, but I knew in my heart, like me, he would have to live with what happened and that is one hell of punishment enough. I felt sorry for him and his family and hoped they could move on from it.

From the investigation into Bernard leading up to what happened, he had sold off most of what we owned or gave it away and the week before he fired those fateful shots, he blew the money on staying at hotels drinking and gambling heavy. I didn't need to know any more, I wanted everything about this to end.

After Bernard's cremation Harry and a brother-in-law were invited back to visit Bernard's family. It was revealed when Bernard was six years old his eldest brother had fired a wooden homemade bow and arrow accidently piecing Bernard's right eye. The parents were not home so the boys placed him in his cot with the arrow still sticking out of his eye and drenched in his blood. This was how the parents found him on arriving home, the father wrapped him in the bloodstained sheet and placed him in the basket of his bicycle and took him to hospital. They went on to say Bernard was never the same after that and by the time he was seventeen he had been in a juvenile detention centre a few times and became too difficult to handle, so his Mother put him on the train to send him to one of his older brothers in another state. He became too much for the brother too. He had a wife and two small children to care for. Bernard had applied for work in a construction crew driving heavy machinery that brought him to the country town, I lived in.

I still ask. Why did they keep such a telling secret from me all that time?

Harry and I never spoke of what happened the night of the shooting, we both had lived it, the memories remain fresh and the scars deep, I am just so grateful that I was able to keep the promise I made to Mum.

We spent a lot of time riding our motor bikes, going for long rides (it was three months before I was able to ride my bike) it was the only time we felt totally in control of our life being on the bike, it was freedom at its best. The road ahead, with the passing road underneath your wheels, and the fresh cool breeze in your face? Exhilarating.

One time we pulled up at a set of traffic lights at a main intersection, and as I put my foot out there was thick oil on the white painted line on the road and my foot kept sliding causing the bike and I to end up laying on the road. We laughed so hard and then we laughed even harder at the fact we were laughing. It was at this point we both began to heal.

Friends made us laugh and slowly we felt like we were back. I went to the hospital for check-ups at first every day for the required two weeks. I swear that nearly killed me, what an effort! On my first visit back I was in the lift with two ambulance officers when one said they were the ones who brought me in that night. That was an incredible moment as I was handed the opportunity to say thank you to two of the people who helped save me. I gave them the biggest hug; they went on to say how good I looked compared to the night they brought me in. My hospital visit continued once every two weeks for a while then every month for three months then every six months. Once a year, every three years, five years and when I had reached ten years, I was to be given the all clear.

The last check-up report revealed there are bullet fragments within the right posterolateral superior chest subcutaneous soft tissues, within the medial aspect right scapula and within posterolateral right ribs space. These could be ferrous and would be a contraindication to MRI. In component these could potentially generate heat and burn injuries. The subcutaneous metallic could be further assessed with a hand-held magnet. There is a bullet tract through the right upper lobe lung field. No metallic foreign body seen within the lung parenchyma. No MRI advised.

I was well on my way. The past abuse and horror was finally behind me. My body was healing, my mind able to think clearer, my brother Harry was doing well, and life seemed to have more good moments.

From here on I could only move forward.

CHAPTER ELEVEN

Stepping Forward in Fear

Six weeks passed when the heavy cast on my arm was removed. I made sure they did not cut though where Doug had written his phone number. This made me think about his offer to have coffee and I knew I would not have to explain anything that happened, making me feel safe. He had chatted about life and had a cheeky smile, so I rang him, and we met for coffee.

Calling Doug was a giant step for me. Part of my traumatic past continued to plague me, leaving me feeling nervous and frightened of some things. Like if a car backfired, I would duck for cover even if I saw kids playing with toy guns I would freeze in fear. I took a deep breath and made the call. Our coffee date was fun and carefree. I agreed to meet again in two weeks. I felt comfortable around him and the fact he had been a policeman for the past seven years contributed towards that feeling of safety.

Doug spoke mainly of his two small children; it was easy to see the pain in his eyes and the sense of deep loss in his voice whenever he spoke of them. His son was seven years old and his daughter five years old. I met them about four months after our first coffee, at Doug's mother's house. They were sweet gentle kids who obviously adored their father and spoke lovingly of their mother and her parents.

As months went on Harry was in his last year studying to graduate as a secondary maths teacher, I was teaching him cooking, ironing and to wash his clothes, in preparation for when he would receive his teaching post.

We still had time to ride our bikes and hang out with friends, but we still lived only a day at a time. I was seeing Doug at least once per fortnight and he told me he was still trying to get sole custody of the children.

I began to notice the same car parked over the road for periods of time. I felt like maybe someone was spying on Harry and me. This thought began to rattle me every time I looked, and the car was there. One day, I couldn't stand it anymore, so I approached them and told them I would call the police if I saw them parked there watching our flat again.

Several days later I received a letter in the mail from the lawyers of Doug's ex-wife asking me to list my assets. I was shocked and showed the letter to Doug. He explained that he was about to go to court for custody and his mother was too old, so he had put my name down as being in the children's life. He said it like it was an obvious thing to do. I was confused and upset. He hadn't discussed this with me, and I knew our relationship was too fresh to even contemplate anything permanent. Doug countered that he was not thinking straight because his head was in the future. This incident didn't sit well with me because he knew I was living one day at a time and not ready for long-term commitment. The shock of his audacity left me feeling unsure about him and I could feel I was withdrawing. He sensed this and assured me he would not put pressure on me.

Six months later, and the doctor said I could look for work, my right arm had lost 10% use due to the fracture of my elbow joint and chest wounds had healed to a point that was manageable. I found a job in a bakery. I had a section out the back where I worked on my own and this felt comfortable and secure.

Harry and I, along with our friends enjoyed our weekend bike rides when the weather was nice. We always loved these rides because we laughed and had a great time. I was happy for Harry that he had the support of these friends as well. Every other weekend I would see Doug and his children, most times at Doug's mother's place. She was of the old school variety where she believed, children should be seen but not heard, a bit too strict for my liking, but pleasant enough. She had seven children of her own and her husband had passed away when Doug was only eighteen.

One weekend after the children had been returned to their mother, we were back at my unit and Doug said we should get married. The way he said it sounded like it was more a statement than a question, so I chose to ignore it. I was not in any hurry to go down that path, it was definitely too soon for me.

Doug was a shearer so away working most times but would be back in the city for most weekend. The year was nearing to an end and soon Harry would know where his teaching post would be, he said I could go with him.

This was his time to venture out and spread his wings, although I would love to have gone with him, but he was going into a share accommodation with another male teacher, I had to be strong and let him go while trying to be positive while feeling the worry and doubt of him venturing out by himself and leaving my protection.

Live for the day and plan for tomorrow was as far as my mind would allow. A few weeks later Doug unexpectedly said, "You never said you would marry me." The only words that came into my head were, "You never asked me." Next thing Doug is down on one knee asking me if I would marry him. My brain careened into overdrive at this point and inside my head screamed a very definite, no!

It was too soon; I was not ready. I wasn't even sure if I had let go of Bernard properly. I felt numb and scared and lost for words. It was under a year since Bernard fired those fateful bullets. Did I still love the man I married but who was the monster he would sometimes turn into, which was real and what was not?

The only person I trusted enough to see my raw emotions was Harry, I had no trust on that level for Doug. I hardly knew him, I needed to heal and then I heard my mouth say, "Yes." I said yes instead of no! Why? I am asking in my mind. Is it fear? Is it the subconscious talking, because the last time I said no, I was shot and so was Mum?

I do not think I will ever be able to say no again. Doug is holding my shaking hands; he never noticed the fear in my eyes or how suddenly the colour had drained from my face. I felt like I had just trapped myself. Doug is talking, and I can hardly understand him, he is saying something about a ring and asking how soon we can get married.

After Doug left, I told Harry and like me he thought it too soon, however Doug had been very convincing, how he would take good care of me, and I would want for nothing and that it would be Harry's home as well. I felt like a scared little rabbit that was looking for a safe burrow to hide in, is that why my subconscious said yes. I know I was not in love with Doug.

One day I had just got home from work and my soon-to-be brother-in-law pulled up in his taxi and said Doug urgently needed me to go to the shearing shed where he was working, to be a cook for just three days until a replacement could be found, as theirs had suddenly quit. John said he would be back first thing in the morning to pick me up and then he drove off. I hadn't even said yes, but I went in and told Harry I was going away for three days and would be back by the weekend. I had done a big shop to stack the fridge and cupboards and told him to get one of his mates to come and stay.

Harry was okay with this arrangement and had been spending more time with his friends. I rang work and said I had to go out of town for three days, then packed and come morning I was on my way to go to the country where Doug was shearing. The farm was called The Hideaway and reminded me of a film named The Hideaway with cowboys in it.

CHAPTER TWELVE

A New job, and a Toothache

It was a two-hour drive out of the city and as we approached the farm I burst into laughter, the Hideaway, I was looking at was built about 1930 and the old grey weatherboards had been painted light blue, but the paint was cracking and peeling. The fences needed repair. The front gate hung crooked on one hinge. What was once a garden was so overgrown you would not try to walk to the front door. Two dogs ran out barking as the car came to a stop and Doug was walking towards us, he thanked me for coming at short notice, as the situation was quite critical. We went in for a quick cup of tea while Doug explained it was Melbourne Cup Race Day (The Biggest Race of the Year in Australia)

The cook had taken his radio to the shearing shed so the boys could stop and listen to the big race, but Doug refused to stop shearing.

The cook became furious as in all the years he had work as a shearer's cook nobody worked when the Race was on except Doug. The cook was so insulted, he took his radio packed his bags, jumped in his car and drove off, leaving them with no cook so Doug was appointed cook and that is where I come in.

There were eleven guys to cook for, I had never cooked for more than five people in total, these guys ate every two hours, and tea (dinner) is a three-course meal. Soup, main meal and sweets (dessert). Doug took me to the shed and introduced me, they all smiled, so that was a good start. Doug had a huge pot of stew on the wood stove already cooking their tea.

He asked me to make two large bread and butter puddings and start a soup. "Can I put my bags away first?" I asked, and we walk through a door right there in the kitchen, the old floor boards squeaked, and I saw in the small room a single wrought iron bed, the mattress was reasonable and an old fashion wardrobe. There was a small window that let in the afternoon sun. Going back out to the kitchen I noticed the big old wood stove, at least I had cooked on one of these growing up with and Mum. She used to love to teach me how to cook and all the secrets to getting the best out of your wood stove.

The wood was well stacked and plenty of it. The huge brass kettle on the stove looked heavy, I wasn't sure I would even be able to lift it, being only 5'3'' and weighing 53 kilos.

The power was on so at least there is a big electric fridge. The work bench was a sturdy wooden table. In the other room was a giant dining table with fourteen chairs around it, I started to feel like Alice in wonderland at the sight of the table.

Teatime, and the guys came in showered and neatly dressed, I soon learned the shearers went by a code of their own, even though tomato sauce was always placed on the dinner table no one dare put it on their food, apparently it was an insult to the cook and certainly no one licked their knives. They were well mannered and spoke without swearing.

I slept well, more out of exhaustion and knowing, I had to be up at 5.am to light the stove and have breakfast ready by 6. 30am.The breakfast menu was cereal, bacon, eggs, sausages, baked beans and toast with a big pot of tea. The hardest part was knowing how much each one would eat, with some coming back for seconds.

As soon as breakfast was cleared away, it was time to prepare for smoko at 9.30am. Thought I would make cinnamon scrolls. They came out looking more like rolled up scones and a bit dry so whipped up a batch of pink icing cut them in half and lathered each one with the icing and slapped them back together. I was nervous taking the smoko over to the shed and quietly handed it over and headed back to the kitchen. When the guys came in for lunch, they all asked if they could have those, delicious cakes again. I wasn't sure I could reproduce a failed recipe twice.

The next couple of days went fast and the guys were great, they helped clear the table, wash/wipe up the dishes and kept the wood pile neatly stacked, they were polite and even told clean jokes, I was a young 26-year-old but felt comfortable because Doug was there. He went back to shearing while I worked in the kitchen. Friday came and the guys all left for home or the pub as soon as the bell rung for knock off, so I didn't have to cook the evening meal. We headed back to the city anxious to see Harry and how he had managed.

By Sunday, Doug received word there was still no cook available, so he told me I would have to go back. We had set the wedding date, which was only six weeks away, with so much to do and plan for it I panicked. Then there was my job in the city that I didn't want to leave and of course I worried about Harry. Doug told me I was needed more as the cook, so I felt forced to tell work I was in the country and could not come back, I felt bad.

Why was I letting Doug dictate to me? Harry said he was managing and had his friends. I ended up doing five weeks as the shearers cook and by the second week two extra workers joined the team so now had thirteen to cook for, which also meant you went on contract pay rate, and was very good money. I think my head was far too busy to even think about me and this gave my mind a holiday from all the trauma.

One morning one of the new guys that was a bit of a prankster came into the kitchen and called me saying he wanted to show me something. I followed him to the toilets expecting to see a frog hiding under the toilet seat which they had been doing, but when I looked into the toilet it was the biggest, fattest longest poo log that looked as if it was trying to climb back out of the toilet and Mike standing in awe next to me saying, "Put some eyes on it and it could be a crocodile.". I felt my earlier cup of tea come back in my throat and gagged as I ran back to the kitchen.

Doug and I never really had much private time while at the farm. I was the first one up and first one to bed, I was quite pleased to be lost in only the thought of what I was there for. Turned out, the guys wanted me to stay as cook. One reason being is the mess bill is divided amongst the team by how much the food bill was per week. I tried to make everything from scratch and the meat and eggs were supplied by the farm, and I was able to feed them well and keep the cost down.

On the weekends, I was able to make bridesmaid dresses for my two nieces and my soon-to-be four-year-old stepdaughter. Doug's sister-in-law, Madge was amazing, she was so excited about us getting married she wanted to do everything. I was truly grateful to her, because of the little free time I had. I finished as the shearers cook nine days before the wedding.

A tooth had been giving me grief, so I made an appointment at the dentist on the Monday, he said the nerve had died and needed to pull the tooth out. He didn't X-ray the tooth and so did not realise there was an abscess under it. He ruptured it and by rocking the tooth and it infected my blood. By the next morning the ache worsened, and the swelling increased on the left side of my jaw. I started to get a high fever and felt unwell. When I told Doug, what was happening he dismissed it and told me it was just bruising and that we were in the summer months, so everybody was hot. Making little sense to me.

By Wednesday, I was feeling a lot worse, and the side of my face had swollen quite a bit more, also under my tongue. I was having trouble swallowing. I went to the chemist who told me to see a doctor immediately. At the doctors, I was told it was defiantly an infection and wanted to inject me with penicillin, after explaining how I nearly died from an allergic reaction to penicillin, he gave a substitute antibiotic. By 11 pm that night I woke with trouble breathing and could hardly swallow. My tongue had swollen so much that it now pressed up on the roof of my mouth and saliva was drooling down my chin. I woke Doug and said I need to go to hospital immediately, he asked if I could wait for morning. I knew I was in a bad way so said I would ring for an ambulance myself. He ended up driving me to the hospital, and on arriving, I was seen to immediately.

The doctor asked Doug why he had not brought me in sooner as I had blood poisoning (septicaemia had set in). I was admitted to the ear nose and throat ward. The doctors came in the morning and things had become worse; they thought the antibiotics would have slowed things down.

By Thursday night, they told me I was dying and best to call off the wedding. I was booked in for surgery first thing in the morning to have a tracheostomy. I told them it was only eleven months before that I was dying of a bullet wound, and if a bullet couldn't kill me, how can the removal of a tooth do it.

They had been injecting high doses of antibiotics into my thighs every four hours and my legs had become bruised and too painful to move. After the doctors left and I was alone, I began to sob and the more I thought how much effort Madge had gone to by cooking and freezing food over the past week. She was doing all the catering herself, and even hand-made four bouquets, she finished making three girl's dresses and set up the backyard to hold the reception in their gardens.

I had to wonder, was this the universe giving me a way out of going through with this marriage? I probably would have cancelled if Madge hadn't done everything and people had already arrived from traveling and to top it off when packing up our unit prior to being in hospital, I came across Mum and Dad's wedding certificate and unknown to me I had chosen the same date they got married, I now started to cry which turned into loud howling. I don't know how long I had shrieked like a wounded animal in the wild, but something burst in my mouth and blood and pus oozed from under my tongue, it was so gross I wasn't sure what was happening.

I pressed the buzzer. Nurses and doctors were all in a flurry as if no one knew what was happening. By now I was terrified and with pleading eyes I was searching the doctors face for answers. After a while he said by crying so hard, I had caused the swelling under my tongue to rupture allowing the infected matter to escape. I was cleaned up and told to try and sleep he would see me first thing in the morning. I woke to being able to breathe better, the doctor came and checked me out saying he was very pleased to tell me I had saved myself from surgery, plus had taught them that in future they just needed to lance the site of swelling. He went on to say three weeks earlier they lost a young man with the same condition and now realized if they had only lanced under his tongue, he would still be alive today.

By Saturday morning I was improving and feeling so much better, I asked the doctor if I could have a six-hour pass for the next day, so I could get married, he reluctantly agreed. I went to get out of bed to ring Doug to tell him but could not stand on my painful legs. The doctor said it was from all the antibiotic injections into my legs. The only way was to walk until the stiffness had gone or use a wheelchair. I started walking around the bed, grabbing hold of the bedding. Believe me I did moan, I had been transferred to a four-bed ward seeing I was on the mend and the other woman were cheering me on, it was so encouraging, I felt like I was walking for all the people who were counting on me to be at my own wedding.

By the end of Saturday, I was walking without support but still very slowly. Doug brought the children in for a visit, and I heard someone ask if they were here to see their mommy which Doug Jr said' "She is not my mummy but will be tomorrow." How cute to hear that, it really made me smile.

CHAPTER THIRTEEN

Marriage and Pigs

That Sunday in January the same day of my parent's wedding day, I awoke feeling so much better, the left side of my face was still swollen but not as much as Thursday. It was 10am and my brother-in-law picked me up, so I could go back to the unit to get ready. I felt weak, my thighs were still sore from all the antibiotics injected into them. The painkillers made my head foggy and I felt somewhat disorientated, but I told everyone I was feeling good.

We had arranged to get married in beautiful gardens that had been Mum's favourite place, where I had been many times to sit with her in the warm sunshine surrounded by lush colourful plants all around us. The time spent here with Mum always held a special place in my heart and why I wanted it to be where I would be married.

We were all dressed and waiting for my brother-in-law to bring the car around when the five-year-old flower girl had fiddled with the wedding rings until the ribbon came undone and my wedding ring fell into the sand, we were all dragging our fingers through the sand until the ring was found. A thought crossed my mind, hoping it wasn't another omen.

On arriving at the gardens, I realised just how far I had to walk and became unsure. I started walking thinking of Mum and Dad all those years ago and how Mum would have been two years younger than me the day she married. This pushed me onwards.

I was feeling like I was acting out a part in a script, doing all the actions. It was pleasant, and everyone looked happy including Doug as he stood there in his pale grey suit with a light blue shirt and a cobalt blue tie. Doug Jr was a miniature of Doug, and the three girls looked lovely in their flowing dresses in shades of pale blue that complimented my gown.

I can hear my name being called in the fog of my mind, realised I was supposed to be repeating the marriage vows. I was so tired. The next few hours were merely acted out in the haze of my brain. Family were saying their goodbyes and I was being helped into the car to be taken back to my unit, so I could change to return to the hospital.

Doug woke me up as I had fallen asleep on the bed and had to be back in the hospital by 4pm to receive my next medications. After dropping me back at the hospital Doug would go back to my unit to leave the ute there and take my Kawasaki to ride to the next shearing shed.

The doctors came in the morning and were making comments about how I manage to go out on a six-hour pass, get married and come back in here with a new name. They all smiled and congratulated me.

It would be another week before I was discharged, I did some quick calculations and cold shivers ran down my spine, both hospital stays were like a repeat. Both times, I was admitted on a Wednesday, nearly died and stayed in the same hospital for ten days.

On being discharged Harry came to pick me up in Doug's one tonne tray back utility to clear out my unit. I was moving to the farm and Harry was moving to a country town to start his teaching position. It was not far from where I would be living, so it was a nice feeling for us both knowing we would see each other often.

Doug arrived the next morning, we had a cup of tea then Doug leaned forward spreading his long arms across the table and said he had things he needed to tell me. He stood up looking down at me and asked me if I believed in the Bible. He knew I did, as this had been one of the topics, we discussed over the last eleven months, I asked him if he could accept my beliefs, as it was important for me to have his acceptance. He always said he accepted everything about me.

His next words left me sinking into my chair as he said, "In the Bible it states that a man is King of his home and when he takes a wife, she shall obey him. So, therefor there shall be no religion in this house! Not now! Or, Ever!"

My heart sank to the bottom of the pit of my stomach and the fear I once knew was back, Doug's eyes had gone cold and, in that moment, I knew I had just made the second biggest mistake of my life. I sat there frozen in fear and in disbelief, he had promised me he would not change anything about me, he had been telling me lies all along to gain a mother for his children.

When Doug left the room and went outside, I sat there sobbing, fearing for my future, my unit was gone, Harry was gone, and most of my money was gone after paying out for the wedding. Everyone was told by Doug to give us money as wedding gifts to buy a septic tank for the new farmhouse and plumbing to connect it. My sister told me on the day after we were married that their wedding present was a septic tank!

Life was manageable because Doug was only home the weekends, and our marriage was more that it filled both our needs. Doug needed both a wife and a mother for the children, and I was happy to do both, because I felt I had somewhere to heal. The farm was only a hundred acres but for me it was perfect. On the weekends, Doug and I worked side by side to build yards and a farrowing shed to start a piggery. This gave us time to get to know each other better and our marriage improved.

Doug had an appointment with his lawyer in the city regarding the custody of the children. I was invited to attend. After listening to the lawyer for a while, it appeared there had been no progress for some months, so I asked him what was the chance of Doug gaining full custody of the children, to which his reply was, "Nil," he said he was following Doug's instruction because he was paying him. We settled on weekend custody with school holidays. Doug was satisfied because we lived about an hour and a half from the city and the children liked the school they attended. It was a win for everybody. Most times, I would drive to the city on a Friday afternoon to pick up the children either from the mother or the grandparents. I found them all likable people and I got on quite well with all of them.

The piggery was now ready. We went to another farm to pick out breeding sows, I had never seen a real pig and in all the movies, they were small and pink with curly tails. I was quite excited until I walked into that shed. The stench was, and the so call little pigs were giant animals with crocodile mouths full of big teeth and worst of all they were free range.

I suddenly found myself eye to eye with a big plump black pig, I was walking backwards while she kept eye contact with me. I had walked backwards into the shed wall and the pig was still coming closer, I thought I was going to be dinner. The owner came running up, smacked the pig on its rump with a "get out of here Susie." The pig kicked her legs out sideways and with a loud grunt ran off. Realizing how naive I was, made me feel quite embarrassed and did my best to be enthusiastic once again.

We started with twenty-five sows and one stud boar. Doug left for another shearing shed on that Sunday afternoon and I had been shown how to get feed out of the mixaul using two large buckets and put it in the feed trough twice per day. Easy enough!

The first morning I was down there and filled the buckets, they were so heavy, I couldn't carry them and the strain on my right elbow that had been fractured would not allow my arm to straighten.

After finding two smaller buckets, I was at the fence and all these big crocodile mouth pigs were crowding around and for the life of me I could not throw my leg over that fence and be torn apart by that savage lot. So, I did the next best thing and emptied the buckets of food along the ground inside the fence while running ahead of them, I fed them like this for the first three days and knew I had to somehow get in there without them eating me. I tried using a broom to push them away while I got the feed in the buckets on the other side of the fence, while the pigs were busy with the buckets; I managed to drag the feed troughs up along inside the fence, ha-ha, now I could just pour it over while using the broom.

It took three weeks for the pigs and I to get used to each other, I knew they only wanted to eat the food and they knew I only wanted to feed them. It wasn't long before I had my favourites and gave them names. I had two Blue Heeler puppies I was training to walk beside me in the pig yard; I was pleased with their progress as they were showing so much promise and gave me much needed company.

Winter would soon be upon us, so Doug applied for a job as a car salesperson in town, which was a fourteen-mile drive. I would still work the piggery during the week and together we would do it on the weekend. I was still driving to the city every Friday to pick up the children. At least with Doug working for Toyota, he had a demo car to drive. One morning he asked if he could ride my bike into work, which was fine by me, however I did think it was strange, as I knew he did not like me owning the bike, said the locals would think he had married some bikie chick. I still enjoyed a ride to remind me of the fact I was in control of my life.

That afternoon Doug came home with a different car, I asked where my bike was, and he said he traded it for the car. I was speechless, there had been no talk about selling the bike that connected me to Harry. How could he just trade it without my consent? He went on to say he had signed my signature and it was already sold. He showed me the papers and the car was in his name only. I went in the shower and while my tears were pouring down my cheeks, the warm shower washed them away. I felt hopeless to try and argue with Doug, I worried he would he shoot me as well.

Another day I was looking for something at the top of the pantry shelf, I came across a tray and some very small packages, one with seeds and one contained some white powder. I showed them to Doug, he told me he had briefly worked for the Australian Protection Board and had kept these packages. One held a lot of seeds to grow some sort of bush called cannabis. I had never heard of them and the other, he said was cyanide.

I was so shocked by what he said he was going to with it. I stared at him and realised he was actually serious! He was talking about pre-meditated murder! I know cyanide is a poisonous chemical gas that prevents your body from absorbing oxygen. The lack of oxygen damages organs and ends your life.

What the hell kind of monster had I married? I kept this in the back of mind, as he carried on as if everything was fine. I was not in the best headspace after this and. over the next few weeks I found out there was a lot more going on. The pigs on our farm were the innocent four-legged variety, but the one I married had two legs.

CHAPTER FOURTEEN

Up in Smoke and Pregnant

My neighbour over the road worked for Community Welfare and suggested I apply for a part time job as he felt I would be suitable. I liked the idea and the next thing I knew I had been selected out of twenty-two applicants for a position with them. This was an incredible boost to my low self-esteem and because the job was only three days per week, I could still run the piggery and drive to the city to pick up the children. My life was very busy, and I didn't give myself time to think much about what was going through my own head.

On returning to the farm a few days after returning the children to their mother, I saw smoke coming from the gully where we burnt rubbish. I could see Doug's ute there. I drove down there and on approaching Doug I casually asked him what he was burning, the reply he gave me sent chills down my spine and that deep dark fear gripped me like a vice that threatened to overwhelm me.

"Your past," he said. "Your life only started when we got married." He had burnt the Birth and Death Certificates for my baby son! It was all I had to remind me that he lived, he also burnt those of my Mum and Bernard's. Everything, all my bike gear and clothes and all my beautiful boots that I wore, now all in flames, my bike sold without permission. I felt stripped of everything I was. I just stood there watching in horror and fear as flames engulfed my entire past. Doug drove back to the house and left me standing there starring into the fire that contained what my life had been.

I felt completely empty of all emotion and identity. Fear held me back from saying anything. I didn't have the nerve to fight back or stand my ground. Since I felt this way and could say nothing about my feelings nor do anything about redeeming my losses, I turned on my 'function only' button and pushed on to survive each day the best I could.

When working the piggery, I wore heavy overalls, high gumboots and a peak cap that I could tuck my long-plaited hair under in trying to avoid the pig dust as this was what made the stench and their poo. They would poo so much in a day. I had to shovel it in a drain that ran down the outside pen areas and then hose them down.

Many a night I sat in that farrowing shed awaiting the birth of piglets with a kerosene lamp to light my way. I had to make sure that the sow did not roll on the newborn while in labour. One sow had been in labour for twelve hours, which I knew, was not normal, so I rang the vet. His suggestion was for me to put my hand in the birth channel, as the first piglet was likely to be coming back first, and not able to pass. The choice was to do this to save sow and piglets or let them all die. So, I am down behind the mother talking her through what was going to happen as if she is a human. I was terrified; I thought she would bite me for sure. I gently eased my hand into the birth channel; the sow gave an almighty grunt, looked at me and laid her head back down as if she knew I was there to help.

I found the piglet doubled over and worked my fingers around to under the chin and worked slowly to bring the head forward. I thought the piglet was dead anyway. I kept gently working its head forward and then out it came, the rest followed rather quickly. The baby piglet was alive! What a relief, not only for the mother but for me also. Delivery time with the sows took a lot of my time but it paid off. I felt very proud.

Days rolled into weeks and Harry would phone me often, then one day he called to tell me he was coming for a visit. I was so excited and couldn't wait to see him and hear all about his teaching job. He arrived late afternoon with one of his mates, who I knew from when we would all go for a ride on the weekend. It had started to rain and knew they would be wet and cold when they got here.

The front hundred acres belonged to Doug's brother, our driveway was lined one side by the boundary fence, and the other side was an electric fence and two main gates. When the boys came into the house Harry said he was backing up pulling the gate open to let Bill in when his wet leather pants touched the electric fence, and he took an arc from it in the seat of his pants. We all laughed visualizing this happening.

I had cooked a lovely three-course meal and we chatted away, while Doug remained rather quiet. As the evening wore on Doug announced Harry was more that welcome to stay with us, but Bill would have to ride back in the rain fourteen miles to town and stay at a hotel. We had plenty of rooms and I protested, but his firm reply was that he did not want the neighbours thinking he belonged to a bikie gang.

I was devastated as I watched Harry and Bill mount their bikes and ride off in the rain. Harry was on a school term holiday and were riding to Geraldton the next day. My heart ached so badly I could not believe what was happening to my life. This was meant to be a new beginning, but I felt more trapped than ever before.

Soon after Harry and Bill arrived in Geraldton, they went to a party, but Harry left early as Bill wanted to party on. It turned out that Bill had far too much to drink and riding his bike back to where he was staying, he lost control and ended up going over the edge of the road and down an embankment and his head hit a tree. In the morning, a motorist spotted him, but he had already died. Harry took this so hard and felt a lot of guilt, but I told him, Bill made the wrong choice to ride his bike knowing he had far too much to drink. Apparently, others tried to stop him too and offered him a ride in their cars. But he had refused.

I saw more of Harry through the first two years of his teaching. His personal life had some hard and challenging moments.

Doug and I had been married near two years when I talked about having a child. Doug said he did not think he could love another child. I knew I was in a loveless marriage and one of fear, but like my dad, I felt like I had enough love on my own for a child.

I decided to see the local doctor because I had not been able to fall pregnant. I was hospitalised for a series of test, but all the tests came back normal, and the doctor told Doug the problem could be with him. The only reason Doug went in to see the doctor was to prove them wrong, but it turned out he had varicose veins covering his testicles and needed an operation to remove the veins. With his manhood at stake, he agreed to have the operation.

The day Doug went to the city for his operation, the farm was hit by a cyclone. I sheltered in the house and when it passed, I went out to see if there was any damage. The stubble that was waiting for a burn off had been cut by the fierce winds; it looked like a lot of it had covered the dam. With a rake, I pulled as much of it out as I could. The rest of the stubble along with the topsoil had blown up against the back-boundary fence causing it to lay near flat. The horse was nowhere to be seen. Three days later it was found several miles away, but apart from that everything else was all right.

Two months after Doug had the operation, I fell pregnant. I was over the moon. I had reached a point that if I only had my two stepchildren, I could settle for that, but being pregnant with my own felt very special. The children turned out to be as happy as I was with the good news. It felt strange to believe I was going to have a baby after eleven years since my darling baby son died. In the eight years I was married to Bernard I had a miscarriage six month after our baby boy died, I fell in a well of sadness for a good long while. But now, I had a good feeling again.

Both families were thrilled when we shared our special news. Doug's mum said she would be happy to do baby knitting and two of his sisters stated they would be making baby things. These blessings caused me to think about Mum and the pink outfit she knitted, telling me on that night that she made them for the two daughters I would someday have. Sharing that moment where my tears spilled on the garment will forever stay in my memory.

At the time of the shooting, my third eldest sister had a baby girl and when they found the pink knitted baby clothes, she assumed they were for her girl. I never told them the truth. I thought they would never believe me and so I kept the secret to this day. I will always remember that special night when Mum told me I would have two daughters of my own. I patted my belly and asked if this was a little girl growing inside me.

My mother in-law had given me her ancient washing machine when we were married. It had the paddle arm with a separate spinning tub. The arm never stopped, and you would have to dive in with your hand one end before it came back to give your arm a wack and it started to shoot flames out from under the bottom near my feet. I shoved it out the laundry door and rang telling Doug to organize a new washing machine as this one was trying to kill me.

With the new washing machine in place, Doug set the old one up at the side of the house, he had been tanning a sheepskin hoping to make a floor rug and it was time to wash it in the old machine. The children were happy playing outside in the warm sunshine, when Doug yelled for me to bring the sheep skin over and put it in the machine. The washing machine was running. Doug, wearing his rubber boots told me to put the skin in the machine. I said "No, I won't do it, that machine tried to kill me." In anger, he yelled the order to do it. And stupidly, I obeyed. I had wooden scrolls on my bare feet, as I was putting the sheepskin into the water, I felt the electricity shoot up both my arms and into my head. Doug just stood next to me and obviously noticed I was shaking all over still hanging on to the sheepskin.

He was about to laugh at me until he saw my eyes rolled back into my head and pulled the cords apart disconnecting the machine from the power. He later said I went flying backwards like a rocket, I had landed heavily on my back and when I came to, I found my lungs cramped tight making it hard to breathe. I was laying on the ground away from the washing machine and the two children were crying asking if I was all right. Doug said I was fine, but I was not and could not move, he had to carry me inside and laid me on the couch.

A few days later I felt like I was in labour, and Doug rang the doctor who arranged an ambulance to pick me up to take me to hospital. I knew I was no longer pregnant, I just felt it. They did a test to see if the baby was still alive but sadly our baby did not survive the electric shook.

The doctor said I could go home the next day, Doug was driving me back to the farm and said losing the baby was like having a faulty design and the next model will be perfect. I cried on and off over the next three or four days, and Doug would say I should be over it by now. I felt angry that he made me use that washing machine knowing it was faulty and then tell me how to grieve and how long I could do it for. I wasn't able to turn my pain off like it had some kind of a switch!

CHAPTER FIFTEEN

A Second Chance

I continued to work the piggery and do my work in town. On returning to work after our loss, there on my desk was a beautiful big bunch of coloured flowers from all the staff, they were amazing people to work with and felt like my family.

Three months passed, and I was sitting in the doctor's office waiting to find out if I was pregnant again. The result was positive, but showed blood in the sample, I was ordered to complete bed rest, which meant Doug would have to work the piggery by himself. The doctor was telling me this baby was going to be the last one he would deliver because he had been diagnosed with cancer. He said he was not going to charge me, and he would visit me out at the farm. What a sweetie, he was only fifty-six years old, the same age Dad was when he passed.

I called work and my boss Jack was so understanding and said not to worry about my job it would still be there after the baby was born and I could bring my baby to work with me. I felt so grateful.

Doug's Mum moved in with us to run the house and feed us, she was a great cook and made the best apple slice. I helped with the light tasks.

I had reached three months in my pregnancy and noticed some of the weaner pig had got out and were biting holes in the hessian lining in the portable silo that held the harvested barley we were about to sell. I could see the grain starting to spill out. I rang Doug at work to come home, he told me to chase them off and he was on his way. I went out the back waving the broom and making noise. They did run away but suddenly I knew I was starting to bleed. My Mother-in-law helped me inside and next thing I am rushed off to hospital, I am trying to stay calm for the sake of my baby and silently telling it to stay strong and hold on.

The doctors gave me an injection and I had to stay in a tilted bed where my feet were higher than my head. The test done three days later came back positive, my baby was okay. I stayed in hospital for a week and when Doug came to get me the doctor laid down the law, that the only things I could do was go to the toilet and a quick warm shower. I could go from the bed to the couch. Otherwise, flat on my back until this baby was born,

Doug sold all the pigs; it was too much for him to handle as he had to also drive down to the city to pick up the children on a Friday and take them back on a Sunday.

The months went by, the baby was growing, and moving, I was happy to feel her, I was convinced the baby was a girl, the doctor came on his regular visits. When I had five weeks to go Doug wanted to show me the adjoining hundred acres we had just purchased. I kept saying I still had to stay inside, but he insisted and brought the ute near the back door, it was only hundred meters away, we got to the gate but instead of stopping Doug started to drive over the ploughed paddock, I started yelling to stop as I supported my large baby bump. I screamed at Doug to think of the baby. He didn't listen.

The next morning, I stayed lying in bed until 10am but needed to go to the toilet, when I stood up my water broke, I was devastated, and I rang the doctor who said to come straight in to see him. Ten minutes' later Doug arrived and started to fill out the heath benefit forms, he seemed to take forever I was desperate to get to the doctor. He knew it and decided then that he wanted something to eat. I told him the doctor was waiting.

We were finally on our way when Doug stopped the car saying he forgot the forms so had to turn around and go back home. It was lunchtime when I got to the doctors, who was about to send someone out to the farm because he was worried something had happened to me. It turned out I had to go through to the city as they had the equipment to deal with premature babies. I wished the doctor would send me in an ambulance as I had lost all trust in Doug because of his lack of care.

Doug stopped at the office to finish off some paperwork, while I sat in the car. I was sitting on a few thick towels because my water was still leaking. I had now started contractions and could not get out of the car. I was doing my best to stay calm as we still had an hour and a half drive. What was Doug doing? I was about to go crazy when he finally appeared. We got to the city hospital, and they question Doug as to, why the delay. I would not allow myself to think what would have happened if my baby was born hours before.

Our beautiful daughter was born at six thirty the next morning weighing a healthy 6b.1oz, after six days in hospital we went home, I could not believe she was mine, I would find myself just watching her sleep and spent every moment cuddling her, I was joyously happy.

When my daughter was nine months old, I found out I was expecting another baby, the two older children were thrilled. There would be fifteen months difference in ages between the two babies. I was fit and healthy and had no problems with the pregnancy and loved spending fun time with my little girl. I was about seven and a half months pregnant when we went to friends' place for a BBQ lunch and there was a new family there that I had not met before, they also had a farm, it was a very pleasant afternoon. On the way home, Doug started talking about how he always wanted a station up north; I wasn't keen on the idea living with two babies in such isolation. He appeared to drop the idea.

I was eight months pregnant and shopping in the heat, feeling grateful that my nice car had air-conditioning, it was a luxury to drive with my little one happily strapped in her car seat. I came out of the supermarket into the heat of the sun, eight months pregnant, toddler sitting in the loaded trolley and standing next to my beautiful car was Doug with some stranger shaking hands. I approached them with a puzzled look and Doug explained this man had just bought my car. My jaw dropped to the ground and my pregnant hormones kicked in making me seriously think about running over Doug's feet as I maneuvered into an enraged burn-out driving off.

The poor bloke was extremely embarrassed when I told him I was not selling my car. Doug assured the person they had a done deal. I was so angry; Doug gave no thought to anyone but himself. I ended up with an old purple and white Holden Kingwood, I probably would have loved it when I was nineteen, but I loathed it. Doug never batted an eyelid when I lost my beautiful car, I was heartbroken. Clearly, this man was heartless.

Doug was always wheeling and dealing about something, he started talking more about buying a station up north in isolation, and I was still against it. Would my reluctance even be a factor in his decisions on our lives? I had many doubts that anything I wanted or needed was ever something he would take seriously and consider.

Two days before Christmas I am about to have our second Baby. It is almost midnight, and the doctor is giving me a choice to have the Baby on the 23rd or the 24th. I like even numbers so at six minutes past midnight my beautiful second daughter is born. I shed a few tears thinking about Mum and could hear her saying," I see you with two little girls," I am feeling so very happy, so utterly complete as I kiss my newborn on the cheek and welcome her. My family is now absolute. Santa visited on Christmas morning and we both received a small gift. On the third day we went home, Doug lifted our first daughter to meet her new sister and gently she stroked her chest and said, "Bubba."

I felt blessed at how much joy these little ones brought into my life and knowing this to be my greatest achievement ever that needed all of me, I never went back to work. I wanted to spend all the time I could with my happy beautiful babies.

CHAPTER SIXTEEN

Moving into Isolation

The talk of buying a station became more frequent. The very thought of this was too far from my mind and my own needs for my children. One child has severe allergies, and the baby has asthma, it is hard enough living on the farm and so far away from a doctor. Doug said he wanted to see if he put the farm on the market for a high price if anyone would show and interest. This made me feel very uncomfortable, but Doug said it is purely an exercise to test the market and simply goes ahead.

An 'exercise' indeed, when some weeks go by, and Doug came home from work all excited about a butcher wanting to have a look the farm over after reading the advertisement he placed. "No harm in letting him look. I will get a feel of what he thinks about the farm," Doug said.

The butcher and his wife arrived, she is lovely but not feeling comfortable with her husband, something about him has my spine tingling. The two men go off to look around while we finish our afternoon tea. The little ones have woken from their nap, and I am busy with them when the men come back inside wanting another cup of tea.

I hear the butcher saying the farm is exactly what they were looking for, but he has one problem, in that he has been trying to sell his sheep station about six hours away from out farm. I am looking at Doug fearful of where this conversation is going, but he is avoiding eye contact with me. He continued to say to the man that we could go up and have a look, and if it's suitable, we can maybe do some sort of swap, where they will still owe us $16.000,00. Again, my jaw hit the floor. It felt like a plan I had no part to play in had been laid. However, I am doing my best to keep my composer. After they left, and we are walking back inside with the children, Doug told me he is planning a trip to this station, with or without me.

A week later we arrived at the station, the day is warm, and the air is dry, the ground is red and there are no tall trees. The homestead is seventy-six years old and constructed inside and out of pressed tin. The main lounge has jarrah dado halfway up the tin walls. No air-conditioning or heating. The furniture looks as old as the house; the linoleum was likely laid when the house was built. The kerosene fridge stands in one corner next to an old wooden table and the same flooring covers a top that served as a workbench. Wooden chairs, aged and worn wrap around the table. The old stove is gas; the lighting is delivered via a bank of batteries.

It truly feels like you have stepped back seventy-six years into the past, except everything had aged to today. The butcher and his wife must be at least seventy years old themselves. There is no way Doug would consider buying this and expect me and the children to give up our lovely new home for this! Surely! Then what about his two children from his first marriage, it would only be school holidays he would see them.

I stopped thinking about the possibility that Doug would take it any further. We stayed the night with no protection from the mass of mosquitoes. In the morning, and even though I had her net over the portable cot, I counted twenty-odd bites on my baby's soft little face, this was unacceptable and just not going to work for me.

But did I have a say? At morning tea, we were all sitting around the old kitchen table and Doug told me that we have a deal. "Hang on," I say. "We, as in you me the butcher and the wife have a deal?" I am politely telling Doug to think on it and wait until we are home to talk more about it, but no, there he is filling out the purchase document. I see he has put my name on it as well, this left me totally puzzled. He bought and sold, wheeled and dealed on cars, my bike, burnt all that I owned, never considered what I thought or said, or to include me, so why now. What was going on, I asked myself.

We left after all the paperwork had been done to seal my fate of what the future would hold. Good or bad; only time will tell. We drive back in silence, except for the chatter the babies made.

Six weeks to the date we move. Doug was in his own thoughts most of the time and I kept hoping the sale would fall through. My fear was for the unknowing of what to expect. Another surprise was Doug had invited a male pensioner in a caravan to live on the farm. This was so out of character for Doug, but he went on to explain that he could move to the station and help him with the work.

I took my babies to the doctor for a general check-up and to let him know we would be moving further into the country to live on and run a station. The doctor told me to get in touch with the Flying Doctor Service in our area, they issue Medical Chest and when in need you ring the nearest hospital and they instruct you as what you need to use by tray number and code, also he would send a letter.

Doug, and Kevin the pensioner, took the caravan and truckload of equipment up a week before I went up with my mother-in-law and the little ones. Part of the deal with the butcher was to leave the farm furnished and we would only take our bedroom furniture and what was used for the little ones. I knew nothing about this right up to the last week.

This was a lot for me to bear and I cried feeling I was always losing the things that mattered as I drove up in the old purple and white Holden Kingswood station wagon.

When I arrived after a six-hour drive with my two little ones and a cranky mother-in-law, I felt exhausted. Walking back into the kitchen had changed nothing from the first day I came here. Kevin was looking pleased as he had lit the kerosene fridge and putting a few things away making it at least look neat. I was overcome with the emotion of leaving behind the lovely home for this, that I just sank into a chair and burst into uncontrollable sobbing. The children were taken outside by their nanna and Kevin was doing his best to comfort me, but at that point there was no comfort. Doug had gone back to the farm for more equipment. I simply felt so distressed that I didn't care where he was.

I had to put the little ones first and got them bathed and set up their cots before bedding them down after they had dinner and a play. Baby Lilly was black from crawling around on the old lino and needed a second bath. She was asleep by 5.30pm and Gabby, my two-year-old, went to sleep at 7.30pm. This had been a long day. The thing that always got me going was remembering when the surgeon said he had to cut through to my lung and could not give me painkillers as I would surely die, my only chance to survive then was to fight.

With this thought I realized I had to fight to survive this house, to cleanse the inside, purge the place of unpleasantness the best I could and give the place a chance to heal from the years of neglect. So, over a cup of tea, I told Kevin that after breakfast we would remove everything in the house including the floor coverings, curtains anything we could lift, and I was going to hose the house inside out, starting from the ceiling to the floors.

Nanna kept the girls busy playing with their toys under the big peppermint tree that provided ample shade. Kevin and I got stuck into emptying the house onto the back lawn, then in I went with the garden hose and sprayed away seventy-six years of red dust and dirt. I noticed the outside laundry and shower had an outhouse like I used when I was six years old, with the cement overhead cistern and the pull chain. I had to laugh, or I would fall in a heap crying.

The washing machine was the next model up from the one that had electrocuted me. I was in fight mode, so bring it on, I filled the washing machine, and it was ready to go. I had to karate chop the curtains to go in the machine, you could not even tell what colour the net curtains were, they were so full of red dust and stiff as a board. When it came time to get the curtains out, I thought they had dissolved. They were lovely delicate lace net curtains which was a pleasant surprise. We cleaned out the kitchen first, I threw out all the lino, even the piece that was on the kitchen table. The actual floors were red Jarrah and in excellent condition.

Once it was all put back it was quite a transformation. I just had to get used to no power and remember to put a kettle on the gas stove instead of filling the electric one.

By the time Doug came back after being away a week, he was more than surprised at how it had transformed.

When it came to cooking, I adapted to the days of when I was the shearers cook, it did take a lot longer to adapt with not being able to use power appliances, and the 4kva generator would run the washing machine but nothing with a heat element. A wood hot water heater was out near the toilet, so there was plenty of hot water. The water had a tinge of colour to it but for drinking water, we had two tanks of rainwater.

By the end of the first week, it was obvious the water pumped from one of the twenty-one wells or bores to wash in, was too hard for the little one's skin, so I changed over to use rainwater and the children's skin and their twenty daily washed cloth nappies were so much softer on their delicate skin.

CHAPTER SEVENTEEN

Life at the Station – Horses, sheep and pigs

For the first twelve months Doug continued making trips to the city and in between his trips, he was trying to cull out the wild horses left on the station. One time, a stock truck carting the horses crashed into another truck transporting cattle to the markets. The roads through the outback were very narrow and with constant wear from the trucks having to move partly off the road to allow other vehicles to pass. The edges of where the sand met the bitumen were eroded leaving a bit of a drop. An experienced driver would slow down and drive the front left wheel off first followed by the back left hand wheel, this would allow the vehicle to be steadier. That didn't always happen of course, and it sometimes sent large trucks adrift or roll over.

Neighbours came to help to round the horses up and take them to the city markets for sale. The last evening, they came back with a young wild black stallion about two years old and put it in the yards near the homestead. Doug said he would de-sex it when he came back from the trip and tame it for the little ones to ride. I knew nothing about horses but did not see how this magnificent black stallion, who had lived his life in total freedom would give in that easily.

Doug did not have time to set up a water trough so told me every morning to take a large tub of water on the bag trolley to water this beautiful animal that had gone yard crazy within a few days. Everyone, even Doug's mum had left for the city leaving me and the children alone in this isolation. The first morning I awoke to see smoke drifting through the trees coming from the South. In absolute fear I called using the old wind-up phone that was a party line to five other stations in the area.

I got through to the fire station, some forty-five kilometres away and asked if there were aware of any fires reported. I told them we had one nearby. They assured me there were no fires that would be of any threat because the strong winds blowing the smoke from a long way away. I felt calmer, but embarrassed for panicking, however, this situation did make me feel vulnerable in being here alone with my two babies. As a result of recovering from the shooting, I obviously still lived in fear of the unknown. I was, after all, still fairly naïve in this new setting which manifested a lot of uncertainties, causing me to often have to think on my running feet. I had to make decisions I felt unsure about and dreading mistakes that in all reasonability could prove fatal.

The next task was to take water to the horse in the small yard. I placed the baby in the stroller, had Gabby hold tight onto the stroller and told her not to let go. I had a filled water container on the bag-trolle.. It was hard going, pushing the stroller with one hand and pulling the bag-trolley behind me through the red, soft sand.

But I got there and discovered, the horse was quite agitated; ears back, eyes wide and fixed on me, tail swishing from side to side and high in the air. The trough was in the middle of the yard which meant going into the yard. With the agitated horse. I reminded Gabby to stay holding the pram. I managed to get to the trough. The horse suddenly turned its back on me, and the hind legs began kicking out towards me. With terror coursing through my pounding heart, I shoved the water off the bag-trolley and held the trolley up to protect myself and got out of there as fast as I could. I quickly took the little ones and secured them in the ute then jumped in and backed up near the gate with just enough room for me to open the horses yard gate.

I knew this black beauty didn't want this confinement. His visible protests told me so. Besides, being a wild horse, he could be a danger to my children. A risk I wasn't prepared to take. Training by Doug or no training, I wasn't going to be party to this, so I casually allowed it to go back in the bush and hopefully he would meet up with other horses to get on in enjoying his natural born freedom.

One day, I found a cow that had recently died from injuries resulting from the truck roll over on the main road. Being such a large animal, I could not bury it alone, nor leave it there to rot because the smell would be unbearable so close to the homestead. The butcher who lived here before us had feral pigs a half mile from the homestead that needed to be fed. So, feeling the only choice I had, was to rope the back legs of the cow and drag it down for pig feed. It was what I ended up doing.

There were two sets of gates, where you would open the front set to drag the feed in, close that set and with a pulley system open the second set to allow the pigs in to feed. My heart began pounding in fear as I began this chore Here was I, an ordinary mum who would go through these lengths, any lengths, to protect my babies.

The savage fanged pigs started ripping apart the dead cow even before I could get back in the ute. I turned and noticed large Bungarra lizards coming out of holes in the ground, their arm muscles huge, their beady eyes on the cow, they stalked their way towards it. I stood and watched as; they had a tug of war with the pigs for the meat. I shivered and went back to the homestead.

There were two forty-gallon drums on the property fitted to what looked like a rotisserie. The drums would be filled with wheat and water, a fire lit under them and the next day it would be turned out into a long pig trough as feed. The butcher killed these pigs and sold them to locals, the thought of anyone eating them made my stomach turn.

The untrustworthy feral pigs were the next to go, Doug asked some neighbours to help. What an event that turned out to be. The pigs literally chased the guys up the raceway and into the truck, one guy lost his shoe in his leap to safety and the pig chasing him grabbed the shoe, shredded it and spat out the soul. I laugh now in retrospect, but nobody was laughing at the time.

By 4am all the pigs that had been loaded on the truck ready for the journey to the city. The seven-hour drive ahead of us went smoothly enough with the children sleeping, one laying between us, and the baby curled up on my lap all of the way. We arrived at the markets to unload the pigs, Doug was about to back up and asked me to hop out to direct him back to the un-loading ramp. I walked to the back of the truck and let out a loud yell when I discovered the added bit of the floor he built to fit the crate had fallen out and so had some of the pigs. I raced back to Doug's side and told him. It was ghastly thinking of how the pigs would have died. I just hoped it was instant.

The first shearing was coming up and we became busy mustering sheep, the ones I saw were old and the number of stock was only about half of what should have been there. The wool was coarse and not worth much, so the first shearing was a disaster. At the end of shearing, Doug and Kevin were drafting the rams off to go through the sheep shower for lice eradication.

Kevin was working the drafting gate when one of the rams went charging up to the gate, but Kevin wasn't quite fast enough, and the ram slammed into his knee, he dropped to the ground, and we ran up to him knowing that would have been painful. Kevin stood himself up and reassured us he was all right to keep working. I really wanted him to go and rest, but Doug dismissed me.

We were invited to a BBQ late that afternoon, Kevin didn't want to go, so I cooked his dinner and left it on top of the stove. When we returned home his dinner was untouched, which is not like Kevin, I begged Doug to go and check on him, but he refused. At 5am in the morning I woke thinking I could hear Kevin calling out in distress, I woke Doug and again asked him to check on him otherwise I would go, I just felt something was very wrong. Doug was straight back looking worried. When Kevin had gone back to his quarters and sat down his knee suddenly ballooned, and he was in so much agony he could not move. I made Doug load him in the car to take him for medical attention. It turned out his knee was a bit of a mess and so he was hospitalised for a time, after which I never saw nor heard from him ever again. I felt very bad that I never checked on him that night, I should have gone.

The old station house.

CHAPTER EIGHTEEN

Nanna Cops My Anger

Christmas followed soon after, Doug didn't celebrate Christmas, hence none of us did. When I was a kid, especially when Dad was still alive, it was always so exciting with heaps of fun. Every Christmas Eve Dad would tell all us kids to go and select a sock from his draw. He would pin our name on the biggest sock we could find, and we would place them on the end of our bed. In the morning they would be filled with all sorts of treats and small toys, we loved this special part of Christmas and I felt sad that I could not give this to my children, but I did the best I could, and both our families spoilt them a little bit. I was so grateful to them.

After the New Year the family we met at the BBQ when I was pregnant with Lilly, were coming to stay for a week holiday. I thought it was more likely the idea of them looking for something different as a place to visit.

Little did I realise, the impact this newfound friend of Doug's was about to have on all our lives. What I didn't know before either, was that he was a major influence in Doug's decision to purchase the station in the first place. Nor the real reason

Doug had changed so much, that I felt I no longer knew who he was; he was so preoccupied in thought and was often back and forth from the shed to the bush. He never talked about the work he was doing, and I was busy with the little ones as my biggest fear was that they would walk off into the dense bush and become lost or fall into one of the open wells near the homestead. I thought if I kept them bare footed, the double gees, a very sharp three-pronged prickle that grew and shed millions of these things around the paddocks, would prevent them from going far.

They were happy and content, playing and laughing and I so enjoyed spending as much quality time with them as possible. Both children handled the heat okay by playing in tubs of water. They were my sunshine and filled my heart with pure love. In return I could feel their love healing all my pain and sorrow of the past. For them I woke every morning with a grateful heart, and I would do anything to protect them. The one thing I wanted them to have, was a stable home with both their parents together.

I soon found out Doug's mother who was in her eighty's was moving to the station bringing her transportable granny flat with her. I was quite bewildered, because I could not see her enjoying this type of lifestyle at all. It turned out it was Doug's idea and he had insisted on it. He always had his own agenda for every decision he made but would never make clear what his underlying scheme was that his decisions were made under until I would find out much later.

Once the granny flat was set up and she settled in Doug fitted an intercom to her bed head and the receiver end fitted to my side of the bed head, where it would go off quite regularly during the early hours of the morning, Doug would either not wake up or pretend not to wake up. It was hard on me as I would be up to the two little ones in the night; the times she would call me were always the same. She felt her heart was playing up; I would take her pulse, which was always perfect. I believe she feared having a heart attack in isolation and I could understand that. I would make her a cup of tea and a slice of toast; she would want me to stay but I would always say I needed to get back in case the little ones woke up as Doug never heard them either.

The second shearing was due, and some months back Doug purchased a truck load of peppin sheep from a farm in the wheat belt area, I had a feeling they were from his new friend. I tried to prevent this transfer because, listening to other pastoralist in the area, they said it was important to buy in your local area as they ate vegetation higher off the ground. Where grass fed sheep only know how to eat from the ground. Made sense to me, but Doug was not listening.

I helped with the mustering as the girl's Nanna and older children were at the homestead, they all helped look after the little ones. I drove the ute, and Doug was on the bike, the so-called work dog, he was given was useless. I soon learned that a top sheep dog could be worth $2,000 or more. This one obviously fell off the back of a truck because at the crucial point where the dog was needed to push the sheep through a gate, the dog ran up front and scattered them instead. I was the one on foot in the heat running like the second sheep dog to bring them back and finally pushed them through. Once yarded; it was easy to see the numbers were poor, most of the new sheep had died as they were still looking for ground feed. We only hired three shearers and I worked the floor picking up fleeces and skirting the wool. We did a second muster as we knew when the dog scattered the sheep, some would have strayed, but all we found was another two hundred. At the end of it all we were at the receiving end of a very a small wool cheque. Another disappointment. The third year following Doug had no interest in shearing. I had to push him to do the mustering and again the numbers were down even more, and because we had taken out an overdraft with the bank before our second shearing was to start, it was Important to keep going.

It was just after the shearing was completed and Doug came back from one of his trips with a 3-day old calf, the girls were excited and called it "Moo Cow" I would have to make up a bucket of milk at feed times and carry it all the way to the shed. One morning as I was coming off the back step with the bucket of milk my left foot rolled on the broken pavement and because I didn't want to spill the milk, my foot rolled quite badly. I heard a snap as the bone in the top of my foot snapped like a twig. I put the bucket down, didn't spilt a drop, but I dropped to the grass holding my leg rolling in agony. My mother-in-law came running, I yelled in pain that I had broken a bone in my foot. Doug had just come down to the house and his mum asked him to help me, he stopped, looked down at me and said, "If you were a horse, I would shoot you."

His mother ran inside behind him and soon both came out, he had agreed to take me to the medical post. The doctor there said, they had no X-ray machine, so if I still could not walk on it in four days to go back. My foot swelled twice its size and was shades of black, blue, and purple and yellow, I could only hop which was extremely painful. When I went back to see the doctor without an X-ray, he said I had broken a bone and plastered my foot up to my knee. I spent the next six weeks on crutches, then I took a chair onto the middle of the lawn and asked Gabby and Lilly to put a hose down the plaster until it went soft and the girls helped me pull it off, we laughed at the fun the three of us had. It was another two weeks on crutches before I could walk without them. Amazing how you adapt to changes and find new ways to do things.

My mother-in-law was becoming hard work, she had no interest, or a life of her own, so interfered in mine, often growling at the children, yelling to get the strap, she had put one up behind the kitchen door. There were times she would come out with the strap in her hand which I would grab from her, she had quite a cruel streak in her. She would follow me around criticizing me in the way I did things. I tried to be patient and understanding, but I knew it was because this was not the life she wanted.

We had just come back from our weekly trip to the nearest town and as a treat, I would let the girls pick out one small chocolate bar each, they would be excited over choosing which one. Mother-in law is following me as I walk my children through the breezeway and begins going off at me for wasting Doug's hard-earned money.

She belittled me for buying my children one small chocolate bar, once a week, and reiterated how I should consider Doug more. Well, I snapped, I looked her right in the eye and told her. "If you think you can do a better job, then do it! Take your son back, cook him all his meals and don't forget he likes a three-course meal at dinner. Care for the children by yourself with no help and it looks like you will be taking your own pulse early in the mornings, because I won't be getting up for you neither will your son. Plus there will be no-one to make you a cup of tea or toast."

With that I held the two little girl's hands and passed them gently to her and turned my back and walked off the veranda and into the bush. I needed my own space, and my own air to breathe, I could take no more from Doug or his Mum, enough is enough!

I walked through the bush with her calling my name and it was only when both my girls started to cry calling out, "Mummy," that I stopped and turned around, the girls ran to me, clinging to my legs.

Mother-in-law said, "You win, I won't interfere anymore." It as a hard-won victory for me because I knew she had already destroyed two or three marriages of her children.

Without explanation Doug started doing a lot more trips to the city. The girls were growing and still happy, Gabby was about to start kindy, and Doug insisted getting a governess. His Mother was doing her best not to interfere, and Doug told her to go back to Perth for six months to avoid the heat.

After he had taken his mother to the highway to catch the coach to the city, he came home and took my hand while the children were playing in the room set up for a schoolroom. With a very serious look on his face, he led me to the bedroom and told me to sit down. He said he was about to do something illegal that did not involve me and the less I know the better. He added that if he got busted by the police, I could slap his face, and then he walked out.

I sat on the bed dazed by the words and had no idea what he was up to, all I knew was I had the children to think of. I did take time to wonder why so much drama happens to one person and if my life was set in some sort of a chain reaction for the string of bad events that seemed to continually plague my life.

CHAPTER NINETEEN

He Shot My Dog

There was quite a bit of activity going on, vehicles passing in front of the homestead heading into the bush where Doug was spending most of his days. I questioned him again and his reply was that it was none of my business, then added with cold eyes, "If you even think about leaving the station or going to the police, there will be a bullet in the back of your head and one in each of the girls."

My whole body froze, and the darkest cloud drifted over me. I fully realised my already loveless life with a spiteful and underhanded control freak would again become a fight for survival. Only this time my children had been threatened and my maternal instincts were on high alert from that second onwards.

How could any father put his family in this situation? I couldn't look at him or let him even touch me, my skin would crawl, and I started to wish when he would go off in his ute, it would roll over and squash him. I never even felt bad thinking this, I had never wished anyone any harm, not even Bernard.

The next time I needed to go to town Doug grabbed me roughly by the arm when I was still on the veranda and my very old, and very protective male Bull Terrier rushed up and grabbed ahold of Doug's calf muscle. His teeth sounding like a chain saw against the back of Doug's leg. Doug whispered to me through clenched teeth, "Call your dog off." I told him only if he let go of my arm, which he did. Instantly.

I turned around and gently ran my hand down Godfrey's raised fur and told him gently he was a good boy. It gave me comfort knowing the dog was there. He had always stood guard when the girls were playing on the lawn, he would even chase the chooks away, he never hurt anything or anyone, but

I always knew if I gave him the command he would. He was the only one in the world right now who had my back.

Shaken by the look in Doug's eyes, the girls and I drove off to the nearest town to get stores and in an effort to not show them my grief, I got them excited in telling them they would be able to pick out their favourite chocolate bar.

Late that afternoon, I was lighting the outside wood heater for hot water, when I felt something bite me on the right cheek, I gave my cheek a rub as it stung and hurt at the same time. I went into the bathroom and there was a red dot, I washed it with cold water and never thought any more about it. By dinner time the bite was burning and felt pain in my whole cheek, I took a dose of antihistamine before going to bed.

At 5am that morning, Lilly came in wanting her breakfast, she was always early to bed and early to rise, I rolled over and saw the horror in her face, she screamed and ran back to her room, I put my hands up to my face wondering what had frightened her. I had turned into elephant woman over night, I could only just see out of slits, I looked in my mirror, and yelled in horror and could see what frightened Lilly. My whole face had ballooned. I raced for the phone to call the hospital and they said take another dose of antihistamine and go to the Medical Post immediately. I had no problem making Doug move quickly this time. If I died there, the police would come to the homestead, so his panic was not about me, but himself.

I grabbed food and drinks for the little ones because we were going to be gone for a while. The doctor gave me an injection of polar amine, and one of cortisone, we waited an hour, and no difference, so another two needles in my butt, thanks, now I had both butt cheeks hurting as well as my face. The nursing staff were amazing in caring for my girls, while Doug paced, anxious to go back to the station. Apparently, I passed out, when I came to, the doctor said my face had gone into white and purple patches, this indicated the medication was now influencing the allergy of the bite. He is then telling Doug he needs to call the Royal Flying Doctor to take me to a city hospital for proper medical treatment, but Doug said I was needed here to look after the girls. The doctor said the girls could fly with me. Doug said a very firm, no. The doctor tried his best, with me also saying it would be the best thing to do. Doug still refused. The doctor shook his head and patted me on the shoulder, saying, you poor girl.

We went home, the girls still too scared to look at me, I slept on a mattress on the floor for twenty-four hours, with really not knowing why I was on the floor. At least after the long sleep. the swelling had almost disappeared. The Medical Post rang to see how I was and gave me an appointment date with a specialist in the city in five weeks.

Doug arranged with one of his sisters to meet the coach and we were to stay with her until we got on the coach to go back. The little ones were so good, but they always were, I felt like I was a very lucky Mummy.

When I saw the specialist, he said I was very lucky to survive such an allergic reaction, the blood test revealed it was Ross River Virus. He joked how women paid big money to get a facial chemical peel and I got one free, I was not amused. It was horrific what I went through in the last six weeks, especially to see your little ones scream and run from you in terror. To hear them call, Mummy, only to run again when they looked at you.

We had been in the city a week and I received the all-clear to go home. Doug rang that night and told me he had to shoot my dog. I held my breath while he said the dog had a fit and could not breathe. I knew he was lying about why he shot my best mate; I knew the reason was because Godfrey had the nerve to protect me against him.

More than ever, I wanted to run away with the girls and never go back. Doug made sure I only had enough money to cover our trip, Doug controlled all the money. It was impossible to go anywhere except back to the demon I had married and too soon it would be time to get back on the coach.

It was midnight before the coach arrived at our turn off, Doug was waiting. Gabby was sound asleep with her head on my lap, and Lilly was in her Bert & Ernie sleeping bag on the floor. With the coach lights so dim I could not see her, and I did panic because I could not feel her anywhere. The coach driver turned on the inside lights, and put over his PA, could everyone please look under your seat for a sleeping child, and she was found still asleep.

Doug and I carried the girls off the bus and drove to the homestead, putting them to bed without waking them.

I was in no mood to talk to Doug, and it was obvious he did not want to either. I felt more trapped than ever and all I could do was go on pretending to be happy for the sake of my girls. They deserved a better life than the one Doug was giving them, he did spend some quality time with them each day, and they loved him so at least I had that. I know he loved them in his own strange way, but that was severely tarnished after he said he could put a bullet in their heads

I was having a hard time accepting Godfrey was dead, he had been so loyal. I can remember back when I got him, after the female bull terrier (Charm) had settled in and she turned out to be gentle and a protective dog.

I was first blessed with Godfrey when I was reading the pet adds in the Sunday paper and a guy was looking for a good home for his male Staffordshire Bull terrier. It had been in the backyard mainly on concrete for 5 years and he wanted a better life for him.

I wrote to him saying I was looking for a male dog to breed with the female I had and would certainly give the dog a good home. He contacted me and came to the farm. He said the dog's name was God, but there was no way I would stand out the back-yard yelling God come here etc. So, renamed him God-frey and he did respond immediately. He was a solid build and brindle in colour, the only problem he had was with my pet pig that I had raised from birth, her mum had rolled and crushed the whole litter and Blossom was the only survivor. She grew up with Charm and would run with her with what sounded like a bark. The first day I had Godfrey she crept up on him and nipped him on the tail. Well, he let out a yelp, turned, saw it was a pig and ran. He appeared very confused over what this pig was. A week later there were some young pig weaners eating the grass in the back yard when Godfrey mounted one thinking it was on heat. The pig squealed, and Godfrey looked down and realised it wasn't a dog and bit the tip of its ear in shame and walked off. It was funny to see, but after that I kept the pigs and Godfrey separate.

I was really going to miss him, he would make me laugh and was gentle with all the children, and he just thrived on all the love. He must have been with me at least six years. Doug always treated Godfrey as though he was some kind of threat to him. I guess it turned out he was, and Godfrey ended up paying for it with his life.

CHAPTER TWENTY

A Warning Shot

It was now time to pick a governess for Gabby and after interviewing several we made the choice of an English girl who had completed her junior teaching degree but missed out on a teacher's posting. She was very passionate about her role, but a bit too obsessive over the school room. The girls loved to colour in and draw in there and knew to put thing back in place, but she would appear displeased which made the girls a bit scared to go in, but in my eyes it was workable.

Doug was still out in the bush every day and there would be a strange vehicle pass the homestead every now and then, Doug and I didn't really talk, it was only when it involved the children, or when they were around, we played happy families, when I

171

gave birth to Gabby I was floating with happiness, and I did promise Doug I would never separate them from him. I felt strongly that I couldn't keep that particular promise anymore. But for the time being, not having much choice I had to play it out.

The Governess got a teaching post after three months of being with the girls, but I was happy to take over. Not long after she left, Doug said he needed to make a trip to Perth but would only be away two days. The day after he left, rain had been falling since early morning and the girls and I were in the school room when I heard like a shot gun go off, the sound came from the front of the house. I pulled colouring books down on the floor with the crayons and told the girls if they finished colouring the whole page, I would give them a chocolate frog each.

I needed to find out why a shot had been fired at the house, so I scurried off on my hands and knees and went out on the breeze way. Constructed with a half wall, then flywire, plus awnings, there wasn't much protection from a bullet. I lay flat to the front and froze in terrible fear. Raising my body slowly to see through the drizzling rain I could see the outline of a male figure holding a gun pointed at the house. My heart was pounding; it was so loud in my ears. I realised who ever Doug was involved with was letting me know they are watching me. I felt sick to the point I wanted to vomit. Had Doug made sure I wasn't going to leave? I strongly suspected he had. My first priority was that I needed to keep a clear head and to keep the girls safe. I made my way back to the school room and the girls were still colouring in. I felt we were so terribly vulnerable.

I am hating Doug for putting us in this situation. We stayed in the school room for hours, it was next to the kitchen, so we had a picnic on the floor and made a camp on the floor in the lounge, even slept in there. Gabby one side and Lilly the other of me, I could not sleep. I managed to lock all the doors and I placed the rifle where I could reach it on top of the cupboard. I checked in the afternoon while the girls had their nap on a mattress on the lounge floor to see if I could spot anyone still watching the house, but there was no one to be seen. They sure let me know they were still there though.

Being shot by Bernard was nothing in comparison to the situation we were now in. The worst fear was, there was nothing I could do. During the night I heard every sound, like the windmill turning, the call of the Mopoke owl, the house creaking as it cooled down. Every little sound heightened my senses to possible imminent danger.

In the middle of the pattern tin ceiling was a décor rose, with open spaces between the rose patterns to allow the heat to escape into the high pitch roof. As it was such a moon lit night I could see quite well and I looked up at the rose. I swear I saw eyes looking down at us. It took all my mind power to convince myself it was a feral bush cat and not jump up and fire six shots into the ceiling and frighten the sleeping children into a seizure. I just wanted morning to come to end the darkness and to know my babies were safe.

In the morning light, I crawled back to the spot where I had seen the dark shape of the person with the gun and felt relieved, he was nowhere to be seen.

Doug arrived back later in the morning and when telling him of what happened, he just added that they also had flame thrower and backpacks filled with diesel, scattered around the homestead in the bush, so if they felt the need, they could easily set fire to the homestead. I had that sinking feeling of being helpless.

During the days I would spend all my time close to Gabby and Lilly fearful for our safety with no one to trust, since my beautiful loyal Godfrey had been killed. It was only during the times both girls were asleep, who were now kept in the same room next to mine, that I would race around franticly, doing as many of the daily chores outside as I could. I saved the inside housework for the evening, once both girls were asleep.

One evening while cleaning the bathtub, I rubbed white powder cleaner all over the inside of the bathtub, I had to crouch inside the tub to do so and when I stepped out onto the tiles my slippery feet went from under me and I fell backwards, I put my left arm out to try and cushion my fall. As I hit the floor my left arm took the impact, and I felt a burning sharp pain just below the wrist. I knew from experience; I had fractured my arm. It was 11pm, but I still went to wake Doug, because I was in shock and pain. Doug half sat up and pulled the rugs over his head and called me some names not belonging to me and that I would have to wait until morning.

I went back to the kitchen to take two pain killers, it felt like there was no support for the bones in my hand and the pain had become intense. I found a small flat piece of wood and struggled to make a splint. To my surprise, Doug appeared without saying a word and finished putting the bandage around the splint, then went back to bed.

Morning bought another trip into the medical post, only nurses available so a two-hour drive to the nearest hospital, where there was an intern from a city hospital doing his country practise. Between me, him and a manual we took an x-ray, which no one could decipher. Many pages later, he did his best to plaster my arm, I tried to tell him to leave my thumb out and use two plaster bandages, not one. He did it his way, folded my thumb over into my palm and using one plaster bandage.

I just wanted to get out of there, talk about a bush wack doctor! Three days later, I was in more pain and had a problem with my thumb under the plaster which had all cracked by being too thin. Back ito the edical post to see the doctor who was appalled by the sight of the plaster. He rang the hospital only to find there was no record of me even being there, and no evidence of an ex-ray film.

The doctor removed the plaster and found I had developed an abscess under the thumb. Again, the doctor is pleading with Doug to call in the Flying Doctor because I needed to have X-rays and a proper plaster applied, but his urgent request to Doug, simply fell on deaf ears, where after more prodding the doctor finally gave in. I asked the doctor to strap my arm the best he could, which took three elastic bandages, and three for spares and we were on our way back to the hellhole. The sling gave me more comfort than the bandages for the next six weeks. The girls were such a great help and so eager to do whatever they could. Lilly loved to feed the chooks and collect the eggs. Doug had filled a 44-gallon drum with wheat for chook feed, and Lilly had gone up to feed them, she must have been playing in the wheat because I could hear her excited squeals as she ran towards me carrying a plastic ice cream container full of hundred-dollar notes. Lilly is jumping up and down yelling she had found a treasure box full of money in the wheat bin. I had to tell her that whoever gave her Dad the wheat also owned the money and we needed to put it back as it was not for us to keep. I told her to go and tell Gabby of her big adventure as it was exciting to share.

My hands felt dirty holding the money and I pushed it back in the wheat as far as I could. When I questioned Doug, his only response was that it was none of my business.

Doug's mystery friend Brett had been for a couple of visits without his family, but oddly enough he was camping at one of the wells, he stated he liked the bush experience. During the second visit he talked Doug into having a huge dam put in where flat ground had a good water run off when the big rains came in the wet season.

The dam was deep and would fill to the top with the rain, we were never going to run out of water. Who or how it was paid for, remained a mystery. I never really saw much of Brett, but this day, on his third trip here, he came to the back door and asked if I could come out on the veranda. He looked troubled and agitated, he went on to say how Doug was involved with some ugly people who were capable of anything, and their activity was involving a huge amount of money where all parties were to take a share each, but Doug had asked for two shares, one in his name and one in mine. I burst into tears and begged and pleaded with him to remove my name as it has nothing to do with me. He went off and I could see his shoulders raised and both his fist clenched,

Forty-five minutes later Doug came in for lunch and kept a poker face like, life is normal, but next I hear someone calling Doug's name and I don't recognise the voice. Doug leapt from the chair and went out as I hear the stranger's voice is angry, very angry shouting out, "I never trusted you, you're full of lies. A man with big mouth. You no good, you bad man!!"

 I froze look while watching through the flywire door. Then the stranger makes a hand like a gun and points it at Doug saying, 'I a shoot man like you, I shoot a plenty like you," and then he vanished. Doug came in white faced and sweaty with his hands shaking, I figured it was time for me to check on the girls and wondered if this was a result of Doug asking for two shares.

After lunch, Doug still looked pale and nervous but was going to check a windmill and asked three-year -old Lilly if she wanted to go with her dad, of course she jumped at the chance as their Dad did not spent much time at all with them during the day. I was surprised as usually it would be Gabby if he did take one of them. They were gone about an hour and on their return, Lilly was rattling on about all these men she saw and cutting down trees. I looked at Doug for an answer, but only got a blank stare before he turned and was gone again.

My stomach turned over and I felt faint, I wasn't sure if I was going to throw up or pass out. I sat on the floor with the girls and rested my head on my knees, my head has images of Doug approaching that very angry stranger who talked about shooting him, while holding Lilly's hand. He had taken my baby girl, to face him using her to save his own skin. I believed Doug would go to any lengths to protect himself and wondered if I had taken the girls and left when he first said he was involved in something and called his bluff, if we would be free off him and this prison. I had realised for some time that Doug was darker than I ever thought possible.

That night I told Doug I was taking the girls on the school camp that had been booked for months. It was near the coast. I jumped at the chance to be away from this prison of the past nine long fearful months. Strangely, he didn't question my reason. So he rang his mother and told her to come back. I found this a little weird, but I let it go feeling rather pleased that we would be leaving.

I was able to move my left arm more and no longer needed the sling, but still had it strapped. My mother-in-law was to arrive in twenty-four hours and the girls, and I would leave the morning she arrived. I'm sure I was happier than the girls about going. I hated Doug even more than I ever thought possible.

CHAPTER TWENTY-ONE

Happy Campers v's the Mafia

The girls and I were finally on our way, and the more distance I put between Doug and us, the happier I felt. We settled easily into the camp. Watching the girls play and interact with all the other children filled my heart with happiness. The freedom a condition in which somebody can act and live as he or she choose, without being subject to any undue restraints or restrictions, made me feel whole as a person and gave me self-determination and a sense of independence I had long forgotten I was entitled to.

Each day that passed gave me a feeling of being in control of my life and as the week was coming to an end, with only two days of camp left, a staff member came to get me because there was a phone call from Doug. His voice was shaky, and he was talking fast but in a low tone, he was saying things had gone wrong and was expecting some trouble, but he just was letting me know. He made no sense at all and had hung up before I could say a word. Even though I felt puzzled by his words, I did not want to pop my nice comfort bubble.

The next morning, I was in a meeting when I was called out to be introduced to two detectives, who told me Doug had been arrested for cultivating marijuana and with the intent to sell. He had been taken to the city and held in the remand centre at one of the prisons. His eighty-six-year-old mother had been taken back to family in the city.

I was told later the police pulled over a ute just before the state border for speeding, the breathalyser test showed nothing even though they appeared drunk. police did a complete search and found they had been smoking marijuana. Further searching found a camera, where the developed photos show pictures of the camp site, dam and caravan. All were later found near the clearance on the property. There was also a note pad in the glove box, and under the concealed floor in the back of the ute were eight and a half kilos of marijuana wrapped in a blue tarp with red soil. Weapons and rolls of hundred-dollar notes were also found there.

The two male occupants of the vehicle were held while the police were busy checking out their findings. On the writing pad the police discovered that there was an indent of previous writing that looked like numbers, a pencil rubbed lightly over the page revealed the phone number to the station. A light plane was flown over and revealed a cleared patch of about three and a half acres. A botanist was called in to analyse the soil found in the ute wrapped in with the marijuana which led them to the station. They entered from the far side, the botanist matched the soil which also proved marijuana had been grown there, and a siege was arranged for 6am the next morning.

My world crashed, and I fell in a heap, I was not able to even think for myself and was being led away by the two Detectives who were saying I had to go to the police station and that I knew why. I broke free of them and turned telling them I had no idea of what they were talking about and demanded they tell me what was going on. They rolled their eyes and said, "As if you don't know."

Now, I was angry and told them I was not going anywhere unless I knew why, by this stage one of the school teaching staff was standing beside me also demanding to know why he felt they needed to take me away. They said I was needed for questioning over the involvement of my husband's activities. I told them I could honestly tell them nothing, so they said I still needed to make a statement. Ben, the staff member at the camp said I had two children to consider, and they told him to arrange care for them. I knew there was nothing I could really tell them so agreed to go.

At the police station, I was led to an interview room where the Detective sitting upright behind a single desk. He was staring at me when he said that I must know why I was there. I informed him of what the other Detectives had said, but unfortunately, I would not be able to help him. He raised his voice and made out Doug had said things about me knowing everything, I stayed calm and said he was bluffing as it was untrue. He stood up and with a louder voice threw more accusations at me and began banging his desk with his fists.

Despite the intimidation, I had no information to share. He said that as a wife I would know there was something happening. I stood up and walked up to the desk and I banged the desk and leaned forward and looked him in the eye as he sat down. I went on to say," Imagine, you love your wife and became suspicious about her seeing someone, but you don't want to confront her as you know then you have to deal with the situation, so you chose not to know, well that is the choice I made."

The Detective relaxed, changed his attitude to a more mellow approach and asked if I was ready to make my statement. Just as it was completed one of the other Detectives came in to say Ken from the camp had come down to take me back to my children. I signed my statement and without any more questions I left. During the ride back, I was shaking and so embarrassed that by now everyone would know, but Ken said he had spoken to all the staff and for the sake of my girls, they would not say any more about it, I Thanked Ken and let him know how grateful I was.

Arriving back at the camp I found my girls and just hugged them, they had been having such a great time playing that they did not even know I had been gone. I made the decision not to tell the girls about their father at this point, they were so happy. My brain was numb, and I allowed it to be that way until morning when camp had come to an end.

Time to pack up, I could not go back to the station, I was scared like I had never been before, not even when I was looking down the barrel of the gun the moment I was shot. I could not face the reality of the whole situation, after ringing my sister I told the girls we would have a week holiday at their Aunty Pearl's, this made them extremely excited as they had a wonderful relationship with my eldest sister, as I did. The news was now out about their father in the newspaper, and I would do whatever it took to protect them in their innocence.

On arriving at my sisters, she took the girls into the lounge to watch TV and we went back to the kitchen eager to talk. I kept waiting for the noise from the TV as I heard no sound, went into the lounge to see them looking at a blank screen and my sister asked them, had they turned it on, to their reply, "We are waiting for the generator to come on." We laughed. On the station we had a 12KVA Lister generator where the first light on would start it and last light off would also turn off the generator. I had to explain how in towns and Cities they had their own power source which went to all houses and no need to turn them on or off by the light switch and promised to take them downtown later to show them the powerhouse. Oh, I so loved them both and felt even more determinate to protect them. With the noise now loud enough to drown out our voices while we could discuss our situation, I told her how Doug had been mixed up with some ugly people who would dispose of people if they informed the police of vital information and left it at that. It was at that point where my brain went into shock and the next few days was just about my girls and keeping them safe and happy.

I could not even think of the next day, I was living in each hour, the fear was terrifying, numbing and all consuming. We had been at my sisters for a week when I received a call from Doug saying he had been released on bail. I don't know for what amount and I know Doug would not have been able to pay it, so who did? He wanted to know when I was coming back with the girls and I realized it was likely the safest place to be and I certainly could not involve my family, it is something I had to deal with on my own. The girls were not aware of anything, I knew the moment would come where they would need to be told and it would be that moment our lives would change forever. I felt pure panic and my insides turned to jelly with dread, I felt like there were no choices, no escape and knew these people would come and find us and if anything happened to my girls, I would simply not be able to live.

I was struggling with the unknown as it was. I could only keep my girls close to me and no way I was going to let their father take them anywhere. My babies, how could I make their lives normal from this point? I took a hot shower where I cried my heart out unheard. I crumbled and sat on the bottom of the bathtub with the shower hitting my eyes washing the tears as they fell. Me wishing it would just do its job and wash my pain down the plug hole with them.

Two days later we were on our way back to the station, the girls happy to be going home and I enjoyed the chatter because strangely, it gave me the strength to face what I must. I owe it to them to keep them safe and loved. I stopped at the town to pick up the mail from the post box. Shirley and her husband Trent worked for the phone company and met up with us. While Shirley was engaged in chatting with the girls, Trent told me the police had been staked out at our homestead and he was told to put a tap on our phone. It was a radio phone with the relay aerial on the tower in town. He went on to say Doug had been involved with the Mafia as the two males who were pulled over were the son and nephew of a man the police had been trying to catch. They couple offered their friendship with warmth and empathy, so that was a comfort because now that I had to face all the locals, it was nice to be told this was not my shame nor the girls. Doug owned this one all on his own. He made his choices with not so much as an ounce of regard to us.

CHAPTER TWENTY-TWO

No Way Out

The months that followed were like being stuck in a nightmare that you can't wake up from, and you know you are living it out. Time was a blur and days simply ran into each other, my insides were still shaking like jelly, and I knew I was having panic attacks as it felt like someone was pinching my nose and cutting my air supply off. I functioned as a mother and even that was a struggle. I could see in my little girl's eyes that they were sensing something was wrong. I was extremely worried about the impact on their future life.

I hated Doug and beyond my natural good nature, and nurturing ways, being a person who is easy going with a live and let live attitude, I wished, with all my being, he would just disappear.

I thought that if he was really concerned for his own children, he would help us to escape from the thugs that threatened us with our lives. However, I had no trust in Doug at all. He threatened us too and I felt like we were more his hostages simply to protect himself. He was as evil as the mafia; he became part of. Albeit, through his own bad choices.

I wasn't coping and Doug allowed me to travel 400km to the biggest town with the girls to see my doctor, I so felt like I was losing my mind. My beautiful sister looked after the girls while I had my session with the doctor, I told him everything from when I met Bernard to what was now happening on the station and the reason why I had to stay. How the fear of what would happen to my perfect babies was more than I could bear, that Doug had threatened me if I left the station, and these thugs would find us.

The doctor stood up and shook my hand and said it was such an honour to meet a woman as strong as me. That after all I had endured, my only concern is the safety of my little girls. He asked me if I would speak at his self-help group, but the timing was not right to do so.

He gave me some self-help tapes on ways to bring back calm, to improve breathing. He instructed me on how to blow in a paper bag when hyper ventilating. He even gave me his private phone number, so I could talk to him 24/7. Along with all this he gave me a packet of medication if my nerves got out of control.

What an amazing doctor, he gave me a lifeline and made me feel I had enough strategies to cope with what lay ahead, the confidence to keep going and to this day I am forever grateful to him.

Apparently, Doug went to the local police and changed his story about who he was involved with. He said it was a small group of unknown blokes who called in and said they threatened him into letting him use our land to grow something. The police already had enough evidence and knew Doug was fabricating new stories.

This stirred up a hornet's nest with the thugs he was really involved with. The phone was ringing, and Doug hung up shaking and pale, he went quiet, then started running around the homestead. He came to me, grabbed my hand and pulled me around, showing me where all the loaded guns were. The ute was parked at the front gate with the loaded .22 rifle behind the seat, he sounded like a crazy man jabbering about expecting trouble that could easily get out of hand and I may need to grab a gun and shoot my way out the best way I could. I was terrified by this time and still had no real idea what was going on nor why.

I stood in, front of Doug and insisted he tells me what is going on! He is rambling about how they wanted to meet him at 8.30pm on some unused road, or they were sending a hitman to do him in. He convinced them to come to the station instead! I screamed, "What about the girls?" He quietly replied it was about *his* life not anybody else's, before turning his back and striding off leaving me standing on my own open mouthed, trying to get a grip on what he just said.

My mind felt like it was in a whirlpool going in all directions, a vortex of confusion, fear, and rage intermingled with how to protect my girls whose safety was all that mattered. Trying to gather some sense of a strategy, I thought the girls and I could hide under their bedroom floor. I had a trap door secretly put in the wooden floor under the carpet. Then I realized there was no way out as it was surrounded by cement and Doug had told me previously that they had placed flame throwers around the Homestead hidden in the bush. We could be burnt to death.

I needed a clear head. I did my calming exercises to think, and the only option I could think of was to give the girls some children approved sedative to help them sleep and place them in a sleeping bag together and I would sit there with them, the minute things turned dangerous I would grab the sleeping girls and run out to the ute and drive through the bush to a safe place. I left the front door open and parked the ute as close to the gate as I could, the keys were in there and a full tank of petrol, with drinking water in the glove box and a bag full of snacks. I didn't care what they did to Doug, as long as my girls were safe.

I can't describe how I was feeling, I don't think I allowed myself to think more clearly. I stayed focused on what I needed to do, how long I sat there just waiting I don't know. I knew there was no point running until they were in the house, so I would know where they were. I hated Doug even more for using the girls and I as his shield. To me, he was a true yellow-bellied coward!

Suddenly, I heard footsteps. It sounded like a few people, and then their voices. I knew the time had come when the voices were raised in obvious anger and became much louder. I was ready to sneak out when Doug started calling my name. I could not believe it! He was actually calling my name! How could he?

I sat there trying to figure out what to do, Doug yelled again; "Jackie, come out and put the kettle on!" I knew I had to go out there, otherwise they would come and find us, and with the girls in a deep sleep, I couldn't risk it. I walked out into the kitchen not looking at anyone, but out of the corner of my eye, at the head of the table was the smooth talker, and one male sitting on the edge of his seat ready for action. There was a fourth male who had his back to me and Doug, who had broken out in a sweat, pale as, his eyes huge and he looked scared. I don't know who any of them were.

I lit the stove and as the voices rose, angry and loud again, out of my mouth came the words, "The police stayed here a week and bugged the entire house!"

It worked, because with that they grabbed Doug and raced out the door. I heard the car drive off into the distance. I turned off the stove and raced back to my babies still sleeping peacefully and sat back down with them. There was no point trying to run I didn't know where they were and felt the house was the safest place.

Again, I sat waiting for the next event, I only heard one set of footsteps on the wooden veranda, no sound of tyres on the gravel and only the soft hum of the generator, no car engine at all. I quietly walked back out to the kitchen to see Doug walking in, my mouth was open, but no sounds came out. Doug began sputtering; "They dropped me off back down the road to walk the rest of the way. I have to drive to the city now! They will be waiting for me at the Airport. They are taking me to Adelaide, don't expect to see me again, I think they will kill me." With that and an overnight bag, he drove off into the night. I turned off the generator and laid at the foot of the girl's bed listening to their breathing and all the night sounds.

I was grateful for the morning light and the girls woke giggling because they were in the same sleeping bag, I told them their dad had gone on another trip to the city and they accepted that without any questions.

There were no unusual sounds or movements around the homestead and three days passed when late on the third day Doug came back. I had very mixed feelings and half of me was extremely disappointed to see him. I was at the end of it and simply couldn't take any more.

CHAPTER TWENTY-THREE

Jailed for Nine Years

Because Doug was soon to appear in court on charges of cultivating cannabis with intent to supply and sell. He began talking to a lawyer. The lawyer told Doug his best chance was to plead guilty to the charge as this would give him a more lenient sentence. I did not attend the court, the girls and I stayed on the station. Apparently, his time in court was brief and sentencing would take place in the city court at a later date.

I asked Doug to tell the girls why he was going away so they didn't need to be lied to and wouldn't need to ask me where he was all the time, but he refused. I decided to attend the court for his sentencing. I sat there by myself and heard Doug continue telling his blatant lies and going so far as to implicate his own eighty-six-year-old mother. Unbelievable!

The sentence was read out, he was to serve nine years in jail. I wanted to feel that the nightmare was finally at an end.

I walked out of the court room alone, bewildered, relieved and trapped in that moment. Making my way to my car, I was accosted by his lawyer and a detective who seemed to want to speak to me. I had nothing to say to them, I shook my head and walked away. Nothing about this case is part of my life from this day forth. No, Doug owned this one. All of it!

Couldn't they understand that I was finally free of having Doug in my presence and in my life. Free of all that he was involved in and free of possible danger of being shot again or my girls becoming victims of murder. It was bad enough they were victims in having him as a father. No, this craziness had been his dangerous game, not mine and I was staying away from anything connected to it. I turned to them and said, "I have nothing to give you," and shaking them off I walked away without looking back.

Life without Doug and his criminal, conniving, cheating ways will be more than better. Hell, I can even buy another motorbike that he can't sell behind my back! That had to be a plus. This was my first chance to be happy with my two girls. As I drove back to where my girls were, I was feeling a quiet contentment with new hope of the start of a new fresh, clean happy life without the dangerous drama and threats to our lives. Without the mental trauma of all that contributed to my life with Doug. I felt like I could now start healing, without thinking beyond life too far, because I knew, the future was still to unfold.

I had little choice but to live at the homestead with my babies. Once back there I realised I was still feeling very unsure of our safety. I couldn't sleep thinking about the flame thrower backpacks filled diesel that would still be surrounding the homestead. I got up and stood watch until near dawn then collapsed into exhausted sleep. I woke again before the girls and walked to the kitchen where I was hit full force with the reality of our present situation:

As things turned out with Doug now tucked away in a city prison for nine years, I was left with $45,000.00 debt with the bank, one-hundred-and-fifty-thousand acres to care for, seventy-two miles of external fencing and the same again for internal fencing. I had twenty-one windmills and water tanks to care for, then the trap yards to maintain There are two thousand-five-hundred sheep that would need to be shorn come October-November. Our power is a 12kv generator with two little girls to home school via school of the Air. The three of us living alone in Isolation would be quite helpless in withstanding the impact this would have on their growing years. And in doing so, I would have to hide so many details about their father from them too.

My legs buckled, and I slid down the wall onto the floor, I put my head between my knees and wrapped my arms over my head and I sobbed like I had never done before feeling totally overwhelmed and worried about how I was going to possibly manage all this alone.

I don't know how long I was there until I heard both the girls crying saying, "Please Mummy don't cry." I looked into their sad little eyes and wiped my tears and stood up hoping I looked at least ten feet tall and said in a very convincing voice, "We are going to be just fine." I hugged them close and knew I would do whatever it took to make everything work out. Feeling a great surge of strength was the same feeling when I lay in hospital and heard the head surgeon tell his team of doctors that he could not give me any pain relief as my only chance to survive was to fight for my life and that is what I was going to do now.

We had breakfast and dressed for the day. It was April the season of wind and drought so it was important to check all twenty-one windmills to see how much water was in the tanks that will supply drinking water for the sheep. There was a pump-jack if needed that will pump water up with a petrol motor. I decided to divide the windmill run into three days to make it more manageable. With water, snacks, kids and dogs we set off on our adventure. Along the way on the dirt track we passed the remains of a dead wild cow when out of its backside popped the head of a large Bungarra lizard. I put my foot down to go faster, so the girls wouldn't be horrified by the sight, but they yelled, "Mum, stop and go back we want to have a look." All three of us had a good giggle as the lizard would poke his head in and out of the rear end of the decomposing cow. I had to give the girls credit. They weren't as squeamish as I thought they might be.

CHAPTER TWENTY-FOUR

Annie Gets a Gun - Loses a Finger

We arrived back in time for their School of Air lesson and before I knew it the day was over. Night arrived and I still couldn't sleep wondering if the mafia would sneak back in the night to do harm to us. I stood in the schoolroom from which I could see through the windows, towards the gazetted road that passed through. I peered in between the louvers listening and looking for any sign of lights. One night while watching, I suddenly saw car headlights, in a sudden panic, I grabbed the louver so hard that it snapped in half. I ran out into the dark stillness of the night, listening to the car motor until it got quieter as it went further away and by then I knew it was travelling to the next station. The adrenaline rushing through my body helped me to stay awake, I think it was always there, only sometimes it would be in the range of low to high. I would manage a couple of hours sleep at the sign of first morning light. Then maybe another two hours in the day.

Feeling tired, overwhelmed but more positive and still feeling that surge of determination, we were ready for our second day of adventures, however a phone call to say a truckie would arrive in half hour to load the forty-foot-long metal shed trusses I had recently sold. I set the girls up in the school room to do some art while the truckie would load the trusses, I told them it wouldn't take long. I walked up to greet the guy and asked if he could use the Massey tractor with the front jib, but he said no he only drove trucks, so I made a deal with him that I would operate the tractor while he used the chains to secure the frames one at a time and get on the back of the truck to steady them into place while I used the jib. I had never done this before so made a deal with the guy to watch out for his own head and safety. The first truss was ready to be placed on the back of the truck and it was going well, it was ready to be lowered to sit flat on the tray back. I moved the lever, but too fast missing his head by a mere two inches, I stood on the pedals and yelled at him "I told you to watch your head. I nearly hit you then!" The poor guy was apologizing, and I was feeling bad. The rest were loaded without any mishaps. I shook his hand and felt a sense of pride for what I had achieved and gave me courage to continue achieving even more.

The rest of the week went smoothly until the weekend when a car pulled up at the back gate with what looked like drunk miners from one of the nearby gold mines. They were offering their services…wink, 'If you know what we mean, love." My ute was parked in front of them, so I reached in for the .22 riffle and they drove off in a hurry. I was shaking all over, it was a new threat I had not thought about, with me and my two little girls living here isolated from anyone, not one I wanted to happen again.

I drove the 45ks with the girls to the police station and reported what had happened, the sergeant seemed to be a kind gentle person who said he would spread word that there would be a regular police car sent out to the sheep station. I, in turn applied for a .22 magnum handgun license to allow me access to the one Doug had purchased. When the license arrived, and I picked it up the sergeant said he would send some of his men into the three local pubs with a warning to not go out to the station as there was an iron fisted woman there who wore a .22 magnum pistol in a holster and would shoot holes in their feet and if that didn't stop them she would shoot their balls off. That was enough to stop the miners coming out.

The police car came at least once or twice per week, and this certainly gave me a sense of protection. How lucky we were to have the police support seeing we're so far out of town. I was so grateful for the extra peace of mind.

We had developed our routine and getting through each hour trying to keep the girls happy and entertained, one time, I sat in the school room with the girls and on a large sheet of white paper, I wrote the word 'Father' then I wrote, 'Mother' then explained that if you take the F of Father and add 'other' taken from the word Mother, you get Fother so when I put my work boots and hat on I am Fother. I then become Mother after I take my boots off. They giggled and hugged me calling out "Hello Fother." It was a bit of fun designed to bring a giggle and it worked. The giggles didn't stop for ages as they made up other names. For me it drew a little line between playing both mother and father to my cherished girls.

Three weeks passed and the chilly winds started to blow across from the dessert. I had enough time to gather wood, split some kindling and light the pot belly stove to put some warmth in the homestead. The girls were sitting at their desks in the school room, I was outside using a meat clever to split kindling when on the last piece, my thought drifted to thinking about using three fire lighteners as it would make the fire burn quicker.

At that moment, the meat clever came down on the side of my finger and chopped off a big slice. I held it up and could see the white bone, I stuck my hand with my finger sticking up like an alien antenna on my head, ran into the kitchen, and wrapped a tea towel over it. I rang the Nursing Post forty-five minutes away to ask for the doctor, who wanted to know if I had the spare bit, but I came straight to the phone in case I passed out. The doctor told me to look for the spare bit, an orderly was on his way to pick me and the girls up.

I went into the school room to call the School of Air to cancel the lessons for the day, the headmaster who was one of our main support people answered and when I said I had lost a part of my finger using the meat cleaver, there was a very loud mutual groan from all the staff. The girls suddenly ask if I had really cut off a finger and could they have a look. I was not game to take my hand off my head and knew I had to go and find the spare bit of finger, the girls followed me outside and I saw the dog chewing on something and felt like vomiting at the thought it could be my finger. As I turned away, I noticed the colour of my nail polish on the bit of finger laying on the path, feeling my knees go weak I sat on the back steps starring at it in disbelief. I reach for my bit of finger and my hand turned to jelly, I had three attempts and jelly hand failed every time. I looked at my four and six-year-old girls in turn and wondered if it was acceptable to get one of them to do it, but the Mum in me said no!!

I found that inner strength and with my good hand reached out and grabbed it, throwing it into the tea towel and covering it over. The girls and I sat on the back step and a short time later the orderly arrived to take us to the nursing post. He asked if I had the spare bit and before I could get a word out the girls both bravely yelled, "Yes she does!"

In the treatment room the doctor asked me to lay down and pulls my arm by my side before removing the tea towel, making the blood start to pump out. The doctor is trying to get a tourniquet around the base of my finger and inject local anaesthetics. I see the spare bit of my finger with nail polish floating around in a bowl waiting to be reconnected. I cannot watch any more, because suddenly my severed finger represented my life and that to put it all together to function perfectly again like it did before, gave me an unexpected insight into knowing my life will never be the same, not now, not ever. This incident gave me cause for reflection.

In the meantime, the doctor is allowing my girls to watch because they are so keen. It appears I am raising two very strong-minded children.

The orderly is standing by, waiting to take us back to the station, the staff have been amazing and very lovely towards us, the three musketeers. My finger is stitched back together, a big fat bandage and sling arranged to keep the finger from moving about. On the way home, the girls are still intrigued about my finger and wondered if the spare bit, as we now referred to it, would grow back. In three days, we would visit the doctor again to find out, during which time new challenges awaited as to how I was going to do everything one handed. I found out that doing things two handed is one thing, doing them single handed, quite another.

A couple of days later, providence provided a blessing. I took a call from a friend I had known for five years. Doug sold them a car through the car yard he was working for at the time and they lived on a farm not far from where our piggery was before we moved. Ben and Rose had a boy same age as Gabby and a girl five months younger than Lilly. They had moved to the city and soon after, their marriage broke down. Now Ben was saying I heard you could do with some help on the station and now he was free with no work commitments he was happy to help out.

I could not believe the timing of this call. He arrived the very next day. Over morning tea, we sat down to draw up an agreement. We both agreed he would work for me with full board, petrol for his ute when needed and once per year in the warmer months when the feral goats would migrate from the north, he would help with that bringing in an income of around ten-thousand dollars. I was bowled over by the fact this was indeed an act of true kindness. This contract would be fixed for two years.

CHAPTER TWENTY-FIVE

The AK-47 Saga

It came time for the visit to see the doctor again. The girls were excited but once the bandages were removed it was obvious, even to me, that the spare bit had died. It was so white against the colour of the rest of the finger and the doctor was saying how sorry he was it had died and that it would need to be removed. I felt the same way I did when my most favourite Aunt died, and the sense of loss to me felt deep, regretful and so very sad.

The girls were taken to the staff room to get a hot chocolate and toast. My finger was again injected to numb it while the stitches were removed, and he tried to pull the bit off with big plastic tweezers, but I screamed in agony due to exposed nerve endings where it had been sliced, He is telling me to give my finger a good hard flick to see if it would fly off. No way this was happening. I could not bear to see it flying off for a second time. With more injections and me not looking he pulled it off. The doctor was saying it needed to scab up and then I would need to be admitted into hospital for a skin graft, at least the hospital was in the town where my two sisters lived so they could hopefully look after the girls.

Leaving Ben to do the windmill run, I set off with my girls to have the skin graft done on my finger. After the surgery I awoke with my sister and the girls sitting next to my bed. I felt like a drunk, making up silly poems to pulling money out of my purse saying the girls looked cold and to go and buy them warm coats, before I passed out. The surgery was a success, and I only needed the one night in hospital. It did take some time for the healing process, where they removed the skin for the graft was more painful than the finger, but the surgeon had done a brilliant job.

The headmaster and staff of the school gave us so much support which gifted me a great deal of relief and comfort. It had been five weeks since Doug went to jail, I had taken the girls down believing it would help them to see where their dad was because I told them he broke the law and had to be kept in jail for some time. The prison was so old and just horrible. I had second thoughts about this being the right thing to do, but how else could I explain it. We were all searched and with metal gates being opened and closed behind us, the clanging and the sound of keys rattling, almost drove me to leave again.

We were placed in a large bare room with a wooden bench-seat around the room, the walls were green like public hospitals walls with dark wooden floors. We were seated with other visitors and then the prisoners were brought out. Doug started pumping the girls about what I was doing, which frightened Lilly who started to cry. I had enough of this debacle, so I said we were leaving and signalled the guard to take us out. I took the girls to a nearby store and let them choose a toy to distract the horrible memory of what had just taken place in that prison. I vowed to myself I would not take them there ever again.

Another week passed and after the girls were in bed asleep, I took a call from a girl in the nearby town who said her brother was in the same prison as Doug. She went on to tell me that a 'hit' had been put out for ten-thousand-dollars to do Doug in and the brother told his sister to ring and warn me as a guy who was already doing a life sentence had taken up the offer.

I felt I had to act on this information due to the fact he was still the father to my girls. I rang a local MP and with all the emotions I could muster, told him and pleaded for the sake of my little girls who had already been through enough, to move Doug out of there and into a minimum-security prison, and that the matter was extremely urgent. The MP pulled it off and Doug was moved to a safer prison. However, he did suffer a few beatings when word got around that he was an ex-cop.

I thought Doug would be more settled, but he was far from it. Being in the different prison afforded him more access to privileges. The prison supposedly had all mail written by prisoners read to ensure they were appropriate, but I received a letter from Doug that read…

"Dear Jackie, I think you should remove the AK47 rifle you have under my mother's mattress.

Signed Doug.

Honestly, I must have read it ten times in fear and disbelief as I knew nothing about an AK47. I rang a close friend who was a police sergeant and read it out to him. While I was freaking out, he asked if I had touched it with my response being a loud no, I never knew about it. He said to get two large plastic bags and wear them over my hands, then put the riffle in the bags and bury it close to the homestead. Then to ring the local sergeant and tell him next time someone is out this way could they pop in as there is something, I need them to dig up.

Twenty minutes later, three police cars came screaming to a halt at the back gate. I raced out and showed them the spot thinking that maybe they thought there was a dead body there, they seemed so excited. The sergeant introduced me to a bank manager who had been standing next to the sergeant when I phoned to talk to him, on hearing my name the bank manager insisted on joining them at the station to talk to me on an urgent matter.

He told me he has had a request from Doug to freeze our joint bank accounts, so that meant I could not withdraw any money. The manager followed me to the kitchen and suggested that I ring my bank straight away to freeze the account, which I did immediately. He then arranged for me to see a lawyer the next day in the city. I shake my head in wonderment and cannot believe what Doug is capable of doing from within the prison walls. How was this even possible? But here it was. Happening.

At 3.30am the next morning the girls and I are off to the city with a six-hour drive in front of us. Our first stop was the bank and then the lawyer to dissolve our business partnership. The Lands Department had rung several weeks ago to explain that Doug was in breach of the Pastoral Lease and his name is automatically removed but my name was still on it, so if I wanted to take over the Pastoral Lease I could do so. I felt because the girls had already lost their Dad, the homestead was the only home they knew, so yes, we are staying. The lease was renewed. The lawyer was a real gentleman around thirty-five or so years of age-, pleasant, warm and friendly, nice surprise.

By the time our session was over I was feeling settled and more confident that I was heading in the right direction and could now get on with planning our future. Before leaving, we spent a couple of days with Harry, his wife and their son, this was a perfect visit before we headed back home. Home. That sounded so good right now.

When we arrived, I hired a governess to school and care for the girls. She was perfect and stayed with us for a year, allowing me to work the station.

I had two-way radios fitted to all the vehicles with the base at the homestead. In the summer months I would be up at 3.30am to get dressed, have breakfast, go out to the shoe room and put work boots on and strap on my gun holster with the .22 magnum handgun before heading for the shed to check that the bikes and vehicles carried enough drinking water and fuel. I then loaded the tucker box with food supplies. My work dog, always at the ready, jumped to and we set off to work.

When the girls woke in the morning, they would call me on the two-way. To have that little chat with them always made my day and helped make me feel stronger in my resolve to keep going, because I knew I was doing all this for them. We would try and be back around 10am when the sun became too hot. This would also enable me to have a pleasant morning tea with the girls and our governess.

CHAPTER TWENTY-SIX

Shearing Day

One morning the police called with a warrant for items believed to have been used to grow the cannabis: On the list was: one tractor, coils of black polly pipe and stand-up water sprinklers, one Robbins motor and several other small items. The police said they would be sold off at the next police auction

I attended that auction because the old tractor had a great post hole digger on the front, which would make fencing so much easier. I swear most of the town folk were there and mainly, as far as I could see, for a sticky beak. I won the bid for the poly pipe and sprinkles to use in the holding yards behind the shearing shed to stop the dust. When the old tractor was up, I put in for the first bid that strangely caused people to start bidding with such earnest that I had to pull out when it got to two-thousand-dollars. Once the bidding was over it had sold for far more that it was worth. I couldn't believe why they thought it was worth so much.

A few days later, the new owner rang me and asked why I had wanted the tractor. When I told him the only good thing about it was to use as posthole digger and was going to use it for fencing. There was silence for about twenty seconds before the quietened voice on the other end of the phone said… "I thought drugs or money must have been hidden in it because you wanted it back." All I could get out was "I'm sorry I…" before I burst out laughing so hard, I wasn't even aware he had hung up.

Soon it became time to start preparing for shearing. I had been involved in shearing during the last three, so knew what had to be done, but it was the doing it which was hard through those sweltering days of heat. I would allow four weeks to trap all the sheep. I had watched Doug truck the sheep up from the back paddocks and there had often been some sheep with broken legs. I tried placing a length of black poly water pipe that would fit below the knee joint to above the ankle. I would cut down the length of pipe and spread it open to wrap around its leg, I was pleased it worked so well.

Each water trough for the sheep to drink from was in a fenced yard and I decided to use the trap system that involves closing the gate, so the sheep walk up a raised ramp made from railway sleepers and jump into the yard to drink, there was no way out. This method allowed us to muster the sheep up to the next level which meant that this would allow easier mustering up to what we called the lane way which ran for seven miles to the holding yards at the shearing shed. I used the hundred cc Suzuki dirt bike, and being only 5'3", my feet had good movement on the ground, so the handling of the bike was light and easy.

My awesome work dog had a wooden platform covered with hessian bagging that provided grip where she could lay comfortably until needed. I cut out the sheep skins to strap on all her feet to avoid burning her feet pads on hot ground and rocks. She was a champion and equal to at least three men on bikes.

I employed two extra local station hands from near-by sheep stations that I knew. My brother-in law had come to help and with Ben and I, a full contract shearing team which consisted of the contractor, four shearers, a wool classer, a wool pressor, two shed hands and the shearers cook. I had a total of thirteen men and six females working for me. I also employed an extra cook for the homestead.

Fuel tanks full, the shearers quarters ready with plenty of firewood stacked for the cook house and hot water heater for the showers. We were ready, and by morning at 7.30am it would be shearing time, everyone had arrived. I was feeling confident although I had expected some of the local pastoralist to contact me for offer of help, the governess told me later that word was around that they thought, who did I think I was? How, as a thirty-four-year-old female could she be thinking she could run a sheep station and a comment about, let's see how long she lasts. This only brought out the fight in me to show them how and strengthened my resolve to prove them all wrong.

At 3.30.am the next morning, I was up to double check everything was in place: After dressing, breakfast, gun holster with .22 magnum around my waist I set off to fuel all vehicles, bikes and filled water bags with fresh water. The yards were full of sheep. 7am I am on my way to the shearing shed when one of the shearers call out: "There isn't enough power to run the hand pieces for cutting the wool". I thought if I turn the revs up on the generator, hopefully that will do, and I see the shearers thumb-up out the window. I think by the law of averages, things run in three, so I brace myself for the next two. Wow, I didn't have to wait long. Ben pulls alongside me and tells me the windmill head fell off during the night where there are two-thousand sheep needing drinking water in their holding paddock. I yell, "Get the pump jack and attach it to the windmill rod. Only one of you need go."

I walked to the shearing shed to welcome and address the team before we start work. Remember there are now thirteen males who will be living here for the next two weeks. First, I take my stance and purposely place my right hand above the gun holster, and I let them know, in no uncertain terms, that I am a very protective mum. So, as I stand before them, I begin telling them the rules in what to do to make working life easier and adding just a few about what they can't do. At the end, they all clapped with a smile. The bell rang to commence shearing, glad I had that task out of the way, we all got stuck into the days work.

Things are working like clockwork until midmorning when the wool presser found me in the sheep yards to say the Robins motor to operate the hydraulic on the press had died, So, as large as life here is the third mishap I half expected. The spare Robbins motor is used on the pump jack to pump water, by the time I got to the shed I had a plan. The tractor's hydraulics could be used for the wool press and so I jumped on and backed it into the loading bay next to the wool press. Yes, it worked. It would do until the Robin's motor I lent to a neighbour was returned to me. I sent one of my station hands to bring it back.

Exhausted and satisfied, I slept for near on two days once we returned to some quiet time The rest of the shearing had gone very well but the sheep were not of good breeding so after shearing, I sold all the weathers, rams and the older ewes and bought in new stock for fine wool and knew I was on a winner. I was feeling good about myself.

CHAPTER TWENTY-SEVEN

I'm Taken to Court

My life had taken on a new calm. I was rested, and with the pleasant sound of giggles from my girls in the school room, came the sound of the phone ringing.

I picked up the receiver to my lawyer in Perth, who quite casually said, "Hi Jackie, you were in court today, it is all okay, because you won." My mind, in a spin, unable to absorb what he just said because I had no idea what he was talking about. He went on to explain he had been served a court summons for me to appear in court from Doug's lawyer. He did not bother telling me as he appeared on my behalf. He knew it would immediately be thrown out of court. His claim was that Doug asked the court to stop me from working the station. I was flabbergasted to say the least, but the Judge did throw it out of court. I found it totally unbelievable that from his jail cell he can do this to the girls and me. It seemed he was free to do whatever took his fancy to try and destroy me in any half-baked idea he conjured up.

It turned out he had a few more of them up his sleeve.

Just a couple of months later, my lawyer rang again with the same conversation. I asked, "What for this time." To which he replied, it was to stop me selling anything from the station, the Judge again dismissed his case.

Another couple of months, same thing, this time asking the court to not allow me to sell his personal truck and massy tractor, which of course, was dismissed like the others.

I started to wonder how many more to come, he had access to free Legal Aid from prison, but my lawyer was costing me money, although, I thought he was worth every cent. I didn't have to wait long to find out. This time, my lawyer rang before the court date which instantly made a chill go down my spine, he went on to say Doug's lawyer had presented a document showing he was presenting to the court asking the Judge to declare me unfit as a mother.

My knee's buckled and I sat on the floor while the lawyer was doing his best to convince me that it will be another one dismissed in court.

I felt sick, threatened and out of control. This came as a major shock and a possibility I could lose my girls. My girls were the only reason I kept pushing forward, they made me feel I could conquer anything. The lawyer was still talking, and I heard him say Doug had arranged a Christian family to take them in while he did his time in prison.

I held my breath and asked who this Christian family was. He said it was my sister and her husband! I couldn't believe this was real. No way would my sister and brother-in-law turn on me like this There must be some mistake! The lawyer said he will attend the court without me and will ring soon as possible.

I rang my sister and asked her why she is betraying me to Doug. She said Doug had rung them asking that if anything happened to me would they take care of my girls. She told him of course they would. I could believe that. What he didn't tell them about was the court document declaring me an unfit mother and what his true intentions were. My sister was devastated and felt so utterly deceived by learning the truth behind his insidious lies. I told her I would ring my lawyer and explain then hoped everything would work out.

Fear still sat heavily in my stomach. Disbelief of the lengths this vindictive male would go to were beyond my understanding of human nature. I cuddled my girls hard and told them I would love them forever and no matter what happened I would always and forever be here for them.

The court day had finally arrived, and I was feeling sick and scared, I scrubbed the stove until is sparkled like a new one. The phone rang but I thought it was way too soon for the lawyer so casually answered and felt dread course through me but then I heard my lawyer's voice. "Congratulations!" he was saying… "You won the case. The Judge read the character references from your bank manager, your accountant, the Lands Department, the principle of SOTA and three of your neighbours. He was suitably impressed and stated that may the court show that Doug be given no further credibility in any court within Australia. And as a further slap on his wrist he ordered Doug to pay for today's court cost and told his lawyer to never bring any issues to any court concerning his wife, as she is providing a stable home with happy children who also had a governess while she is holding down a good business and being a valuable member to the community."

My lawyer is convinced that it is now finished, it is done. I was floating high with his stupid unfounded threats no longer going to be an issue.

I settled my account with my lawyer who to this day I am indeed grateful. He did an outstanding job for me and my darling girls.

Getting back into our daily routine felt good, but I wasn't convinced that Doug would let me live trouble free and again I was right. It didn't take long before he was up to new deceitful tricks.

Russel from the Lands Department rang me after speaking to my accountant because he received a letter from me to be presented to the board for a decision regarding me asking for permission to destock the station.

I was blurting out that the letter did not come from me. That I had written no such letter and why would I want permission to destock the station? I'm busy trying to upgrade stock, improve the business! He went on to say my accountant had told him about just coming back from the station after doing my tax and how I was planning the station's future.

I sighed in frustration and asked Russel to always ring me and confirm that I wrote any letter that comes in from me. He agreed, and all I could do was hope that Doug will one day give up these feeble attempts of trying to ruin me.

It was obvious Doug had written the letter and signed my name, he did the same when he sold my motorbike, then my nice car while I was shopping when I was about to have our second baby and there were other things as well.

Doug had let slip years after we were married how my first husband's mother had written to me when he and I were first married. It was a letter to congratulate me and said she truly wished I had found real happiness and how she would love to come and stay for a visit. Doug wrote back signing my name stating how I had no desire to ever see her or her family ever again. I cried about how evil this act was, I cried for the lost opportunity to stay connected and how she must have felt to get a response like that.

He went on to say "Oh, that is not the only one I got rid of. Remember the four-year-old boy you fostered with Bernard? Well, when he was eighteen, he came to the station with his dad looking for you while you were in the city. Well, I sent them away telling them you had no wish to be in contact with them again because you had a new life with me."

Evil, evil man! how could any human being with any decency do this, and ruin other people's lives without a care? In my mind only a truly malicious Narcissist is capable of being this nasty to someone they said they wanted to marry. I guess, in retrospect, he saw me coming. A perfect victim who had already been to hell and back. Doug had been extremely nasty behind my back from day one and I never saw it. I tried to track the boy and his father down but to this day, I've had no luck finding them. But one day I will.

I was furious, and the hardest part was that I never had the chance to ring Doug and question his actions while he sat in his cell. I doubt I would have received a straight answer anyway.

A few days went by whilst I continued to shake my head at all the trouble Doug was causing. I was about to put an order through for windmill parts to Southern Cross, when the phone rang. A woman asked if I was Jackie, I said I was and she went on to say she had received my letter and I had been approved for emergency housing near the prison so the girls had easier access to visiting their father in prison. My tongue has gone so dry I found it difficult to form words, my mind is spinning, why does this woman think it is me? I searched the ceiling and knew. Doug!!

I was able to calm down and asked her to read the letter out and this confirmed for me it was Doug trying to still get me off the station. What I still find unbelievable is that apparently the prison read all mail going out so how is he getting away with fraud in the prison system. I found out later that if I had spoken to the prison Security, they would have put him on a security list, and I could have charged him with Fraud.

Surely there is nothing left he can do to me, but before too long I was in for another one of his surprises. Friends from near our farm before we bought the station rang me asking if they could come and stay with us for four or five days. I was happy to have them there because I really liked Shirley and Bob. The girls were also excited about then coming.

 The mother-in-law still had her unit there, so I was able to prepare it for Shirley and Bob. They arrived with lovely gifts for the girls and took the time to talk to them showing great interest in all that they did and the girls gave them a very proud tour of their school room. They showed them their work and a few drawings they done and invited them to the school room in the morning to listen to their class on the radio. I felt my heart fill with such pride for them both in helping to make these friends feel so welcome.

Bob and Shirley shared meals with us and asked many questions about the running of the station, it was so nice to be able to share so much with them and the next morning after the air lesson I was able to take them to some of the windmills and show them all the improvements I had made.

We had lunch with the girls, and they asked if I would take our visitors to our secret cave for a picnic lunch, seeing as the next day was part of the weekend. We were all happy and really enjoying their company.

On the third night of their visit, I had just curled up in bed when I heard them talking through the intercom. What they said was my next surprise. Bob is saying to Shirley that the girls and I are all so happy and thriving here on the station, there was no way he could do what Doug asked of him to try and talk me into walking off the station after I destock it. Shirley cuts in with a stern, "Don't you dare! They are very content here and doing well. Tell that Doug to leave them alone."

I turned off the intercom. I hadn't realized it was left on. I buried my face in the pillow and sobbed heart wrenching sobs, the purpose of their visit was instructed by Doug. I had a rough sleep that night and woke with a heavy heart, but put on a brave face when they came in. We had breakfast with the girls doing all the talking and giggles, then they were telling the girls how it was time for them to go back to their farm. The girls asked them to make sure they come back to which they assured them they would.

As I walk them out to their vehicle, Bob gave me such a huge bear hug then looked me in the eye and told me I should be very proud of myself for doing such a grand job with the girls and the station. Both are saying how proud they felt of me and assured me that I had their full support, one hundred percent. In fact, they would arrange next time to bring up all their six adult sons and they would all chip in to help out.

WOW... my heavy heart did such a leap to joy. It had been eighteen months of endurance and back flips since Doug first started to try and remove me from the station, the thing is, even if I did destock and just move somewhere, there was no chance whatsoever that the Lands Department would ever let him work the station again. I wonder if he ever realised that or even if he cared. Perhaps his only aim ever was to try to destroy me after all.

CHAPTER TWENTY-EIGHT

Things Come in Three's Again

I had reached a point where I was now convinced that Doug had to have run out of options, at least for the time being. Surely. So once again, we all settled back into our happy routine. Ben worked hard and long hours we kept making improvements and upgraded the homestead. Fencing was an ongoing project, we put in a new goat run with a new holding yard out further in the bush but had chosen the flat ground below the rocky outcrops, we knew the feral goats came through there. At this point I had taken on extra casual help as it was the season to think about shearing time and the goat season would be starting after that. The underground tank between the cook house and homestead had been fibre glassed and a new dome shaped lid was made for it with a small flip lid on the side. I was feeling proud about this as the windmill pumped fresh clean water into the fifteen-foot-deep tank.

Mustering the sheep was almost complete, the sheep were in two large holding yards and only need to bring mobs down to the shearing yards. My neighbour had gone away on a break from the station and left her horse in the paddock next to the cook house. We were ready and by mid-afternoon the contract team were stating to arrive. I was feeling lucky this time around.

At 2am in the morning I woke to the sounds of what sounded like an animal plodding water, this was not unusual as we have had a stray goat in the swimming pool. The water depth was over five feet and we found large lizards and other wildlife had come for swimming lessons too. The splashing seemed more intense than I had ever heard, so I grabbed the torch and went towards the pool but I realised the plodding sound was coming from the back of the house. Heading towards the sound I was quite confused as to what it could be. I was near the new underground tank and waved the torch light over the lid and blow me down, suddenly a horse's head popped up through a big hole in my new lid. The flight mode kicked in and I yelled to the horse, 'Stay there, I will be right back." I ran to the shearers quarters and ran the torch butt along the wall made of corrugated tin and yelled to the shearers as loud as I could, "Put your pants on and come out here, don't think just follow me." Within minutes ten sleepy men rolled out, while I am yelling out orders. "You get the rope in the maintenance room, you, bring the tractor over here, and the rest of you follow me." I lead them to the underground tank and was explaining that any second a horse will pop his head up out of the hole, and "Tom you need to wrap your arms around its neck and hold on no matter what and the rest of you need to make a human chain, so the horse does not pull Tom under the water, it is 15 feet deep!"

The tractor with the jib was on its way, I could hear the shearer who had gone to get the rope was running back, and the cook had put a few outside lights on. Next thing the horse reared its head, I could see it was tiring, Tom and all the guys leaned back and I'm yelling, "Tom throw your arm around its neck," which he did just as the horse started to go down dragging Tom headfirst under water, I'm yelling again to the guys to grab Tom's legs and make a human chain and pull with all your strength.

The tractor and rope had arrived. I quickly made a noose and tired one end of the rope to the jib, as Tom and the horse came up, I got the noose around the neck of the horse. One guy is yelling that I will strangle the horse to death, but the way I saw it was better to die above ground rather than at the bottom of 15 feet of water. I signalled to the tractor driver to raise the jib and yes, up came the horse and we all helped to swing it around to stand on the ground. I am cradling it head stroking it using a calm voice. After a few minutes, I saw the horse widen its eyes as it looked at me and noticed his ears go right back as his lips part to lunge at me for a good bite. I started to run with this big horse right behind me, thought the horse and I were friends.

I'm running around and around this tree with all the guys laughing. I suddenly stopped to face the horse with both hands up and said the magic word "Whoa boy!" miraculously it stopped, so did the laughter. I gave the horse a slight flick on the bum with "Get out of here." and it happily trotted off. Except for my pride, and the damaged new lid on the tank I was no worse off. We will have to pump all the water out and start again, but at least the insurance would cover the damage.

Was this the start of things that seem to run in threes? I hoped not. The third day into shearing one of the shed hands became ill. I needed a replacement, so I rang the Employment Agency, there was a young male there and I was able to speak to him. Asked if he had sheep experience and could he handle working in the heat which he said he did and was very keen to learn. I picked him up from the coach stop in the morning and he went straight to work. I gave him a list of instructions and where things were, plus the other shed hand would be his work buddy. I always make sure they understand how important it was that in the heat they were not to put ice blocks in their water bottles and not to guzzle when they drink, as it was a sure way to end up with bad stomach cramps.

I came back three hours later to check on him, only to find him outside doubled over and vomiting with stomach cramps, he had done all what I asked him not to do. He went to lay down for an hour, then came back to fill the shearers shed pens with sheep. Watching him reminded me of the dog Doug bought but ended up always scattering the sheep. I pulled him aside and asked what sheep experience he really had; the answer made me laugh as he said his uncle had a pet sheep to eat the grass around the house. On asking him if he wanted to stay, his firm answer of no, meant I had to drive forty-five kilometres to put him on the next coach. He was a pleasant kid and said he learnt to always be more honest on his work experience but had also found out he could not work in such heat; we were averaging 42 degrees centigrade out there. Not for the squeamish. I paid him for a full day's wage and farewelled him wishing him all the best, one of my local guys ended up filling in.

Since I had brought the poly pipe and sprinklers, they were working perfectly to keep the dust down in the sheep yards behind the shearing shed. Now it was time to bring up the rams to go in the shed for shearing. I called my work dog, but as she came into where I was standing in front of the rams, she was rammed quite hard knocking the wind out of her. She ran behind me and started barking at them with her head between my legs. I am giving the command to get around behind them, which normally would see her jump on the back of the first one barking as she ran along the backs of them, pushing them all forward. She was obviously still recovering from the brunt she got. Next thing a big ram came charging, the dog took off and before I could step aside, I was rammed by it, knocking my feet backwards and I did a spectacular full-face-plant straight into the mud. Everyone in the shed came out to witnessed my face plant. What could I do? I did what any Aussie would do, I rolled over laughing in the mud, feet in the air doing a wiggle. I stood up and took a bow. It was good to share a laugh.

Next thing the shearers are pointing behind me, when I turn around, I cannot believe what I am seeing. My male apricot miniature Poodle, a whole fifteen inches high, is running up to the rams and as he goes underneath the middle row, he nips their ball sack and has them running up the ramp into the shearing shed.

Everyone dashed to their workstation and shearing was back under way, a big hooray for the Poodle, who became the talk of the station for many days to come. It's unsurprising that these little dogs who weigh between twelve and twenty pounds are often circus trained. They are smart and adaptable and easy to train making them a very popular breed. I loved my new untrained sheep dog.

Happy to say, the shearing continued without any more dogs getting bulldozed by rams, horses getting into the water tank or boys that couldn't handle the heat.

CHAPTER TWENTY-NINE

The Cook House Burns Down

The shearing task finally came to an end, the rams are droughted into a paddock where they will be fed lupin grain as a supplement to their diet while held until the mating season starts. The ewes are spread out in different spelling paddocks. The wethers, which are the castrated male sheep are loaded for the markets and lambs have been tailed, to avoid fly strike. The male lambs are castrated by using a disinfected ring applicator once the lambs are secure in a cradle. This is the safest method.

Young sheep found with even one black hair are placed in the meat paddock. When the wool is tested before the sales. Each bale is core-tested, and it only takes one black hair to lower the value of the whole bale. So, it's not good business sense to neglect checking this otherwise small detail.

With all the sheep handling completed, the work pace is much calmer. We usually end up with visitors wanting to stay, an elderly couple we know, Sheila and Shaun loved the bush lifestyle, they phoned to say they were arriving the next day. I arranged that they would be set up to stay in the cookhouse for their visit.

That night as I slept, I had a very unusual dream, it was in snapshot photos. I saw Shelia and Shaun having dinner with us, then an almighty whoosh sound and the governess screamed my name from the laundry. Flames at least twenty-four feet up in the air came from the cookhouse, the next shot was me putting sleeping children into the back of the Landcruiser. I woke up in a panic when I had seen my children. I lay puzzled, frightened and trying to delete images from my mind. Thinking this is crazy but couldn't shake of those images.

At breakfast I sat down with my giggling little happy girls, joined by the governess and Ben. I gave a nervous laugh and told them all about in what I had seen in that the cookhouse burnt down in my dream. I left out the part about the girls.

We all laughed loudly and were all in a happy mood. First thing after breakfast the cookhouse kerosene fridge needed to be fuelled and lit. On asking Ben to do this I held my five fingers in front of his face and clearly said to fill the fridge tank with five litres of kerosene in the tank. I repeat this several times as it is important not to overfill, especially after my dream.

By late afternoon Shelia and Shaun have arrived to the delighted squeals of the girls. We were about to sit for an early dinner because Lilly was always in bed soon after. I invited them to join us and would help them unpack later. We finished the meal, the girls were asleep in their beds, and we were chatting away, while the governess had gone for a shower in the laundry.

Then just like in my dream, we heard the loud whoosh of the flames. The governess is screaming my name. Racing out on the veranda against the black sky the twenty-four-foot flame was coming out of the cook house. I ran in and saw the flames traveling all over the ceiling, the chemical smell was so chocking, I yelled to get out now. luckily Shaun had not unloaded their ute so their things were safe.

When I asked Ben how many litres of kerosene he put in, he said eight not the *five* I had told him repeatedly. He was responsible for turning the kerosene fridge into a bomb.

I quickly rang the Fire station which was forty-five kilometres away only to be told I was out of their territorial jurisdiction. I explained the cook house was only fifty meters from the homestead and the breeze was blowing directly towards us. The chemical smell was bad, we were worried about sleeping children. The Fire Chief was amazing, he said to load the children into a vehicle and get someone to drive them up the road to a safe distance. The Landcruiser seats were set up as a bed from our previous trip. The girls did not even wake up, they were used to being moved around while they slept. The Fire Chief went on to say they could take the old fire truck out of the museum and see how many volunteers he could get and will be out there soon.

Meanwhile, we have hoses spraying water on all the tamarisk trees along the back of the homestead fence. My firefighting trailer is twelve miles away where we are fencing as we recoil the heavy wire from the five-line fence, to reuse it we throw the wire in a fire, then rethread it as it has become soft. The tractor is used to pull the tension on it.

The old fire truck arrives, I would laugh only my kneecaps are sliding up and down out of anxiety. The water hose is run out to the cook house, I see one guy chopping a hole into the new lid of my fiberglass tank. I cringe a bit then I race over yelling, what are you doing, he replied they were trained to do this to access the water, I flipped the lid next to his feet and the guy with the submersible pump lowered it into the water. Meanwhile there are three men on the hose yelling, there is no water.

The fire chief is at the front of the truck trying to prime it for the water with a crank handle. Two men on the hose leave one there, to go and give the chief their suggestions. The water come through and the guy on the hose is yelling "whoa! woo! woo! We look around, the gorged water hose is lifting him off the ground. The guys all run to help. Some are pulling the tin off and soon the whole wood frame of the building has collapsed into burnt charcoal.

Four hours after the fire started, it was now out, the children were back in their beds. The fire fighters all sat down on the edge of the concrete, exhausted. We all were, fatigued from adrenal and the intense heat. With me now thanking my hero's and looking at their blackened, exhausted faces. It was, by now, after one o'clock in the morning.

The governess came out with snacks and an iced beer that I sent her to get. There was only one beer each and in no time, we are all laughing about the hole in my new tank lid. Another insurance job I needed to explain. We yelled three loud cheers for my hero's then another three cheers for the fire truck out of the museum. What a night.

In the morning I am on the phone to the insurance company putting in a claim. I am talking to Glen who is the supervisor for claims. I told him about the kerosene fridge blowing up the and the cook house catching alight, then how they had to bring the vintage fire truck from in the museum out, and the fire fighter who had to chop through my tank lid, Glen is laughing so hard he can't talk, finally he says, "Jackie' each month we have a pick of the funniest claim and your horse falling through the lid is on the office cork board right now, none have been able to beat it, but this one sure will."

I can see the funny side to both claims, let's just hope there are no more. A cheque was coming in the mail to replace the cook house for the shearers cook to work in and a third lid for the underground tank.

Ben, Tom and I are on our bikes back to where we left off fixing the fencing. Years before, when I was nineteen, Bernard taught me how to ride a dirt bike in the sand, this proved to be helpful nowadays.

Shirley and Shaun like doing their own thing, but today they are guests in the school room with two very happy young girls. The governess will serve them all lunch. We have our own tucker box for our lunch, and the fencing is making great progress, when I smell goats in the wind. Big male goats urinate all over their under carriage and boy do they smell. If you are down wind, you will know they are there before they are aware of you.

On yelling "Goats in the wind!" We down tools and revving up our bikes, headed into the wind. The large herd of goats are just ahead of us. Tom will ride behind them; I will ride along the left side, and Ben will ride along the right. Our aim is to guide them to open flat ground and run them along the fence line into the holding paddock.

All is going well until a big black billy with wide horns breaks away in front of me, I yell to tell them I am going after him. When I manage to get alongside the goat, I kick the bike gear into neutral and turn off the key as I'm reaching with my left hand to grab the horn on the left side of the goats' head and throwing my left leg over the goats back. as I let go of the bike which is by now not far off the soft sand to land on its side.

It is an instant adrenaline rush as well as a huge challenge, but as they say, practice makes it easier. I am now on the Billy goat's back holding on with both hands to his horns, next thing the goat is arching his back and my feet have gone forward making me lean back as I pull his head up, he is in control and heads for the bush. Tom yells, "See you next week". I manage to sit upright and push his horns forward making his chin rest on his chest, he slows down, and I am back in control. When the goat can't see ahead, he slows to a trot, and you simply steer him like a motor bike to a mulga tree.

We have hay binder twine looped through our belts so when we have the goats head up against the tree, we pull one off and tie the horn from one side around the back of the tree to tie off on the second horn. The bush track is close by, and I break off a mulga stick to mark the goat's location. I join Tom and Ben and we have a smooth run getting the heard into the holding yards. Ben goes back to get the ute parked where we are fencing, to pick up the billy tied to the tree and put him in the holding yard,

We let two neighbours know we are catching goats as we need to fill a triple decker semitrailer, before we can order the truck. The sale of the goats to the Middle East will be money towards Ben's income.

CHAPTER THIRTY

Last Stands

The months go by quickly and it's already time to start thinking about shearing again. This shearing round I decided to use a new holding yard now that the fencing has been replaced and has so much sheep feed in it. We are underway and so far, no mishaps. We have the same team, and all feel comfortable working together and for that I am grateful. Ben has been there almost two years, the contract he made with me was for the two years and after shearing will need to discuss where we go from there.

We have done our first week of shearing and all is well. My friends in the nearby town have installed a new backyard pool and I have been invited to a cocktail party to celebrate. It is on a Sunday night. Ben and the shearers are telling me that it will mean a long weekend as I won't be fit to work on the Monday morning. I laugh it off as I won't stay long, and I don't drink alcohol. I purchased a gorgeous above the knee cocktail dress, I am so excited to finally dress up like a woman and feel a million dollars in my black and white chic flouncing skirt, little black cocktail hat with black stilettos. Hair and make-up done, I promise Ben I will be back before midnight to be there and get up at 3.30am to muster the two thousand sheep from the new holding yard. No idea why he laughed,

Once at the party there is a cart with a guy making cocktails, they look just like fruit juice and tasted so good. There are so many different ones to try. I am having the best time with all my friends until someone tells me it is midnight and time for Cinderella to leave.

I get to my car and head for home. My head feels like it's in a different place and I suddenly change my mind, I decided to go back to the party and pull into a service station car park. I am in my small car, dressed to impress.

I fail to drive forward or backwards and decide to get out when I fall to the ground. I have never been drunk before. I see now, that to mark the parking area in the Service station, they lay down telegraph poles and I have somehow managed to drive my car to belly up on the length of the pole, all four wheels are hanging over the edge going nowhere. How on earth did I manage that!

I need help and at midnight I am strolling down the dark deserted street, my clicking stilettos are the only sound heard. I have no idea where I am going, but lucky for me the police pull up and ask what I am doing. I am trying to explain that my car has bellied up on the post. They help me into their car and drive to where I *parked* my car. On seeing it, they are both indulging in a big belly laugh. It takes both police all their strength to get my car back on solid ground.

The police made me drink a bottle of water and escorted me halfway back to the station with the promise that I must ring the police station once I am home, which I did.

The alarm went off at 3.30am and I dragged my body out of bed and off on my bike to muster the sheep down to the shearing shed. I am acting on instinct and thought I was doing so well, until Ben pulls up and yells at me asking what I am doing, to which I reply I have done three corners and looking for the gate near the fourth corner. Only to have him yell that we are in the triangle paddock. Oops!

Ending up with only eight hundred sheep instead of two thousand. I give in to defeat and declare a half day holiday, so I can sleep off my fuzzy head. There's a first time and a last time for most everything, I did both in one day, I won't be drinking ever again. The police came out to check on me and still laughing, told everyone about my carparking abilities. I figured that this was my three mishaps in one.

The rest of the shearing is completed smoothly.

Feral goats are coming through so have done the first big catch. Ben is now saying his contract has ended and wants me to make him a partner on the pastoral lease. I am so shocked and unable to believe he is being serious; his attitude has changed. The next day he was going out to truck the feral goats into the homestead yards. Lilly is excited and begs to go with him as she has done many times before. On return Lilly comes into the kitchen with a little baby goat in her arms, saying Ben said if she got in the yard with the wild goats and caught it, the goat was hers to keep, she was so proud of herself. I was not so happy that she was placed in danger. She was only seven years old.

I told Lilly to take her baby goat to the shearing shed and I will be up to help put it in one of the pens. I had only just walked out the back gate and heading to the shearing shed when I saw Lilly covered in blood and carrying the head of her baby goat by its little horns. While trembling, she keeps repeating that Ben had cut the head off while she was holding it.

My protective mother instincts took over and I removed the goat head from her. She was in such shock and as I wrapped my arm around her, I kept promising that I will fix it and found the governess to bath her while I took the bloodied head into the shed. Ben started laughing and I threw the head splattering its blood all over him and then I pulled my .22 magnum pistol from my holster and aimed it at his chest with the hammer pulled back and my finger on the trigger. He is now yelling saying I was f...ing mad. Oh, you bet I was, and my finger a hair away from pulling that trigger.

The only thing that stopped me was the thought I would be in the same prison as Doug, and seeing his smirking pleased smile. That thought stopped me. I could not leave my girls.

I released the cock pin and looked at my watch, I told him he had ten minutes to pack his gear and remove himself from the station. I would wait by his new four-wheel drive and when ten minutes were up, I will shoot holes through his car and he would have to explain why it was full of bullet holes.

He took seven minutes and thirty-nine seconds before he spun the wheels and I watched him head for the main road I made him a promise, that if he came back, I would shoot holes in both his feet.I sincerely meant it.

It was another three years before I found out Ben had taken mafia money to work there for the two years. Why, I never found out, but I had my suspicions that Doug had something to do with it. From here on I knew I couldn't afford to trust anyone anymore.

I had placed an advertisement in the paper hoping to find a capable worker, to replace Ben. Two days later I spoke with a male who seemed very keen to take on the role. I drove to the city to interview him and his wife. They said it is their dream to work away in the bush and already bought a large caravan to live in. I explained it was not a fairy tale lifestyle and would be hard work. I needed to explain to the wife that in the summer months her husband would have days where we start at 4am and if she was the jealous type then it would be in their interest not to take the job on. They would live in isolation and with power not being 24/7, she would have the use of the laundry and shower. When the children finished school hours she could engage with the governess and the children. I would ensure they were comfortable as possible. I gave them a week to really discuss it, they rang to say it was what they really wanted to do.

Once they arrived and had a couple of days to set up, they were aware I had given them four weeks trial. Seeing it was our quiet time there was no real early start and we would be checking windmills and some fencing. I knocked on their door for the first day of work and he comes out wearing thongs and holding a .22 riffle. I reeled back in shock, once I have composed myself, I ask if he is ready for work, to which he replied, Yes.

First, you cannot work in thongs, and you certainly do not need a rifle. He reappears with his good black dress shoes on. It was all he had. We got through three weeks, but I knew it was not going to work for either of us. They decided to leave in two days' time. I wished them well and with the wages I paid him, they would have a holiday before going back to the city.

Lucky for me a friend on a station nearby had a niece and her boyfriend looking for station work and had experience. My Governess was also about to leave, it was recommended to me to only retain them for twelve months, so they don't get overly complacent nor too attached.

It was now time to really think about the future and what is best for the girls. Doug was due to be released from prison in eighteen months. I made an appointment with the prison superintendent so I could discuss when it would be a suitable time to divorce Doug. The girls were excited to be going to stay with my eldest sister.

Sitting opposite the prison superintendent I am asking him about divorcing Doug, I really want to do it when it will be the easiest for him. To my surprise he is saying, "Do it now, while in prison we can watch him and if he needs to have someone to talk to, we will get him help, also he will have time to adjust to knowing there is no future with you."

After all Doug had done, there was no future at all for him to be with us. The superintendent is still talking, and I am hearing his words, saying I still seem uncertain, and he picked up the phone to see if the prison councillor is available to see me. Next, I am led to his office, and he also told me I needed to do it now. I was Doug's life raft, but he was still trying to pull me under. "Cut the rope and set yourself free." he said.

He gave me the card for a Marriage Councillor and offered me the phone, she said she can see me right away. After an hour session with the marriage councillor, she tells me to come back two o'clock tomorrow as she would like go to the prison and talk to Doug.

Next day back at the Marriage Councillor, she rests her head on her arms and slowly looks up and says in a slow voice, "Only God alone can help that man, there is no human on this earth who can. My advice is to divorce him and shut him out."

I now have an appointment to see my lawyer first thing in the morning. What I thought would be a quick visit with the prison Superintendent, has turned into a series of appointments. Sitting opposite the lawyer I am telling him to serve the divorce papers on Doug in prison. I walk away knowing I have done the right thing.

That evening at my sisters, the girls were snuggled into a comfortable sleep. I hear my sister on the phone and tells me it is the hospital, and they need to talk to me. The person on the phone is saying that Doug had just been admitted to the hospital showing signs of having a heart attack and is asking for me. I went to the hospital and Doug is asking who I am, something doesn't feel right, the hospital have decided to fly him to the city, and someone will ring me in the morning.

The morning phone call is from a psychiatrist at the main city hospital. He is telling me that Doug is perfectly healthy but does deserve the Global Grammy Award for the best take off for symptoms of having a heart attack, he has such control over his brain he can release a chemical to fake a heart attack.

The country hospital sent him to the city as they could not detect anything wrong with him. The psychiatrist went on to say, they were sending him back now. He said Doug would try it again and when the hospital rings, tell them you will not be coming in to see him and wish him well. He will recover quickly as it has not had the effect on you as the first time. Doug did do it again and recovered quickly when I did not visit. I was evermore convinced that Doug was nothing less than an evil narcissist.

CHAPTER THIRTY-ONE

Plans for the Future

I have sat the girls down to discuss our future and said it will soon be time to sell the station and move to the country town where my two sisters live.

Doug has a cousin who has been visiting him and recently rang me telling me Doug was planning on hiding out down the furthest windmill when he is released from prison and will wait for me to come to check the windmill. He would then shoot me and drop me down the well and take over the girls and the station.

I do believe Doug is capable of anything and it made me realise that I need to sell the station and move to the country town where the prison and my family live. It would be the safest place to be.

The selling Agent has arrived after my phone call to him, regarding listing the station on the market for sale. I drive him around while I talk and drive, he is taking photos and notes. By late afternoon he is handing me the pen to sign our agreement.

This is a difficult choice for me, because I feel I belong here and after all the hard work, how can I just walk away. The thought of Doug's threat and the girls having to go to boarding school if I stay, made me wonder how I would protect them if I'm not close by.

I sign the contract with a heavy heart, but know it is the only good choice I have left now. After the girls went to sleep, I went out to my office, broke down and cried. After dialling the agent's number, I hear myself begging him to not put the property on the market after all, that I need more time to think this through.

Two weeks later, I know I have to think of the future for me and my girls. The looming threat hung heavy in my mind and considering what Doug has done to me so far, I couldn't give him the opportunity to finish me off now that I had come so far, done so much and needed to be around to take care of my girls. So, I called the agent and told him to put the property on the market. I added, that should I at any time ring him, and no matter how much crying or begging, he had to promise he would not take it off until it is sold.

It is strange how in the beginning living with Doug and moving to the sheep station was near indescribable. I very much opposed to buying the sheep station and then I was trying to work out how I could escape with the girls during that very dangerous time, to now having such trouble leaving.

I felt quite distraught about leaving here. I made this place what it became. Once Doug was in prison, I found new strength as a mum and a woman to take on huge challenges that I never thought possible.

This man I married, this ex- policeman of seven years, the one who promised to keep me safe and love me until death do us part, was a pathological liar. All his treachery, the greed and out for himself attitude without remorse or regret for whom he hurt on the way right down to his own flesh and blood daughters is still unfathomable to me. He is a con artist of the worst kind. Everything I first believed about him was nothing more than a lie. Everything. And it took me a very long time, a great deal of physical and mental abuse, going back to my first husband to realise the truth.

The terror and pain I endured over these years is beyond what an ordinary woman can sustain. Beyond what an ordinary man can inflict on another. But I did endure.

I did suffer and I did make my way through the survival of all this.

I had been played to the cruellest degree. Suffered years of mental torture until I submitted and felt utterly worthless and lost my identity.

I fought back. I fought back hard to be a better, stronger person, to become a survivor and to feel proud of myself and hopefully allow the girls to believe in themselves.

I fought by working hard, taking a stand, brandishing my gun when I needed to and began to be able to tell people where to get off. I learned to stand up for myself.

It only took six weeks, and we sold the sheep station. I bought a house near a beach. I know we will be safe there.

Gabby and Lilly are excited and on our way to a whole new life.

This may seem like the end of my story, but there is a brand-new chapter about to start for us. Wish us well.

■■

Thank you for reading the story of my life. It hasn't been easy writing it because the raw emotions come back to the front of my mind as I re-live these horrors to a degree where I often need to stop and take stock of my feelings.

This is my story, one of survival, and of a strength I never knew I had.

It took me a very long time, a great deal of physical and mental abuse, going back to my first husband over and over again to realise the truth of our marriage, but Bernard and I were very much in love with each other, and I had clung to that.

Bernard who had a mental illness gives you some explanation to his behaviour. The terror and pain I endured over those years is beyond what any woman can survive. Beyond what an ordinary man can inflict on another. But I did survive. I did suffer and I did make my way through surviving the shooting and all that entailed.

In contrast, during my second marriage I had been deliberately played to the cruellest degree. I suffered years of mental torture until I submitted and felt utterly worthless. In trying to just survive day to day, I lost my identity, my spark.

But I fought back!

I fought back hard to be a better, stronger person, to become a survivor and to feel proud of myself and allow my girls to believe in me, and in themselves. I fought by working hard, taking a stand, brandishing my gun when I needed to and began to be able to tell people where to get off. I learned to stand up for myself.

AUSTRALIAN OUTBACK KNOWLEDGE

The Outback

Basically, the outback is usually inland Australia, a long way from the sea. Exactly where the outback I starts and ends, can be difficult to define. A place that is astonishingly varied, alternately lush and bountiful and dry and barren with wide open land, a sea of stars above and a place that can be both harsh and dangerous.

The outback epitomises all the remote areas that lay way beyond the city lights. The outback is where red dirt, low bushes, sparse trees, huge ant hills, flies by the millions and dirt roads reside. With a spattering of farmhouses and acres of farming land that exist in this environment, it can be unforgiving and sometimes cruel.

Kangaroos, foxes, wild dogs and cats, camels, snakes, goanna's, lost cattle and sheep and all kinds of other animals both pre-domestic and wild roam the countryside in search of food and survival.

Windmills

Windmills have graced the Australian skylines for more than a century, they had become a vital component of rural life, pulling water up from bores and wells. They are still a stronghold of this inexpensive low maintenance method of watering stock. The head of the windmill can vary in size up from twelve to eighteen feet in diameter. It is essential to regularly check on the working of the windmill to ensure stock always have water.

Shearing Sheep

Shearing is seasonal and annual. The timing of fly strike risk, lambing and the availability of shearers must be considered as part of the decision-making process of when to shear. The weather is a keen factor, looking at the start of hot weather and before thunderstorms are due, avoids loss of sheep due to maintaining their body heat once shorn.